Wild Goose
big book *of*
worship resources

Wild Goose
big book *of*
worship
resources

**wild goose
publications**
www.**ionabooks**.com

Published 2017 by
Wild Goose Publications
21 Carlton Court, Glasgow G5 9JP, UK,
the publishing division of the Iona Community.
Scottish Charity No. SC003794. Limited Company Reg. No. SC096243.

ISBN 978-1-84952-531-2

Cover photo is a derivative of a public domain image created by Aaron
Burden, licensed under creative commons by stocksnap.io
https://stocksnap.io/photo/FO2E9T2CQJ

The publishers gratefully acknowledge the support of the Drummond Trust,
3 Pitt Terrace, Stirling FK8 2EY in producing this book.

Overseas distribution
Australia: Willow Connection Pty Ltd, Unit 4A, 3–9 Kenneth Road,
Manly Vale, NSW 2093
New Zealand: Pleroma, Higginson Street, Otane 4170, Central Hawkes Bay
Canada: Bayard Distribution, 10 Lower Spadina Ave., Suite 400, Toronto,
Ontario M5V 2Z

Printed by Bell & Bain, Thornliebank, Glasgow

Contents

An infinity of stars

Daily prayers for Advent

Jan Sutch Pickard

A word about these words

There are so many biblical texts associated with Advent. The daily lectionary gives us several different ones to be read each day. Recently I tried a different discipline: to take just one text at a time, preferably one that recurred over several days in the lectionary, and to spend time with that one passage. Reading and re-reading, living with it, reflecting on the images it brought to mind, the down-to-earth human experiences, savouring words with particular power, or the way the passage evokes times and seasons in the place it came from – the hills of the Holy Land – or in the place where I am now, a Scottish island. Suddenly I found I was responding with my own words. Not many words: brief prayers which were some-times exclamations and sometimes poems of just 17 syllables, a rough-and-ready version of the Japanese haiku. So here, starting with a text for the days leading up to Advent Sunday, is a stumbling, wondering journey through this season in which we prepare for 'the Word made flesh'.

Thursday

Psalm 25:1–10

Winter sun rising red,
wild geese in flight:
in you, God, I put my hope.

Friday

Psalm 25:1–10

Frost white on the grass,
dawn footprints:
teach me your ways.

Saturday

Psalm 25:1–10

Evergreen shelters small birds
feasting on berries:
tender care and constant love.

Week 1

Sunday

Psalm 25:1–10

Blackbirds call down the dusk:
set down your failures,
end the day forgiven.

Monday

Psalm 90

Oh satisfy us at daybreak
with your love,
that we may sing for joy.

Tuesday

Psalm 90

You were
before the mountains formed;
we shake in the wind like winter grass.

Wednesday

Psalm 90

Winter thunder
startling with its anger:
our secrets bared in a flash.

Thursday

Luke 1:68–79

From fear, from those who hate us,
from anger that consumes us,
set us free.

Friday

Luke 1:68–79

Children lost in a minefield:
walk with us God, peacekeeper,
guide our feet.

Saturday

Luke 1:68–79

We longed and waited:
now the contractions have started:
deliver us.

Week 2

Sunday

Luke 1:68–79

Darkling God
in your tender compassion
break upon us like the dawn.

Monday

Psalm 126

Rain in the hills,
waters roll down,
stones of the dry wadi dance and sing.

Tuesday

Psalm 126

We sowed, doubting
anything good could grow;
now we laugh: grateful, amazed.

Wednesday

Psalm 126

Frozen drops hang on birches like tears:
breathing the pure air –
we're alive!

Thursday

Isaiah 12:2–6

We run before the storm,
reach a shed, rain drums upon the roof –
refuge.

Friday

Isaiah 12:2–6

Midwife God,
encourage us, parents-to-be,
to grow in confidence.

Saturday

Isaiah 12:2–6

Clear the spring
of dead leaves, mud, ice,
so water flows freely – deliverance.

Week 3

Sunday

Isaiah 12:2–6

On that day mouths will sing,
savouring good words –
comfort, confidence, joy.

Monday

Isaiah 11:1–9

From the felled olive tree's root
a new shoot springs:
God's resilient life.

Tuesday

Isaiah 11:1–9

Strange companions –
no more predator and prey –
in God's transformed world.

Wednesday

Isaiah 11:1–9

Curious, lively children,
unaware of danger –
God, keep them safe!

Thursday

Psalm 80:1–7

Lowering sky:
shepherds on quad bikes gather flocks in-bye*
before the snow.

Friday

Psalm 80:1–7

Long nights, short days,
oppressed spirits:
God, let your level light shine on us.

Saturday

Psalm 80:1–7

Austerity – scraping a living –
stale crusts:
sorrow our daily bread.

Week 4

Sunday

Micah 5:2–5a

Waiting for the due date,
blessed by anxiety and hope:
bring us peace.

Monday

Psalm 113

Brief winter's day: from sunrise
to sunset may all we do, God,
honour you.

Tuesday

Psalm 113

Glimpses of glory –
the merry dancers in the midnight sky
praise God!

Wednesday

Psalm 113

God's economy:
the rejected find dignity,
the poor, justice.

Five more prayers based on
readings for Christmas

Luke 1:46b–55

Frost-defying, heart-warming:
the steadfast beauty
of winter roses.

Luke 1:46b–55

God, your name is holy
and your mercy sure –
lifting up the lowly.

Luke 1:46b–55

Fresh bread, dhal, chicken soup,
maklouba –
God fills the hungry with good things.

Micah 6:4–8

What shall we do now?
Love mercy, act justly,
walk humbly with our God.

Isaiah 9:2

Midwinter midnight, deep darkness:
then – look! –
an infinity of stars.

** 'In-bye': sheltered land surrounded by a wall,
rather than rough grazing out on a hill*

Advent signs

Prayers, reflections and
symbolic actions

Glendon Macaulay

This series of prayers, reflections and symbolic actions can be led by several voices. Some old clothes, a baby's feeding bottle containing milk, pieces of a broken wine bottle (handle these carefully) and a lit candle should be set out for all to see. Individual communion glasses can be used for the water, milk and wine.

John the Baptist

Responses:

Leader: People of God,
            what are we getting ready for at this Advent time?
All: We are getting ready to receive again
            good news about the Kingdom of God.

Leader: Why are these old clothes here?
All: They are a reminder of John the Baptist,
            who did not wear expensive designer gear –
            and was not a flashy dresser!

Leader: And what is there to sing about in this Advent season?
All: We sing our songs to celebrate that, when the time was right,
            a man called John the Baptiser came to clear a path,
            and point beyond himself to Jesus, the Christ:
            Child of Bethlehem; Man of Calvary;
            God Incarnate; Love Divine;
            the Living Love of Heaven on this earth.

Reading:

The man called John the Baptiser came from where he lived in the desert. There, he existed on a diet of locusts and honey, and was dressed in what amounted to no more than rags. In many ways, he was a weird kind of guy – something of an oddity, if truth be told. But he was certainly a charismatic character, and folk flocked from miles around to hear what he had to say. Without doubt they were moved by his powerful words and fascinated by the message those words contained.

John told them about a life-changing kind of personal baptism: a baptism of God's full and total forgiveness. He said that if individuals were prepared to acknowledge they were essentially flawed; if they were willing to admit that a lot of the time they didn't live their lives in accordance with God's intention; and if they were truly and truthfully sorry about this; then he would baptise them in the River Jordan. This, he said, would have the very real effect of wiping the slate clean as far as their previous wrongdoing was concerned, and they could start life again. More than a few took him up on his offer, and jumped at the chance of a completely fresh start.

Some of these folk thought he was the long-awaited Messiah, but John was at pains to point out that nothing could be further from the truth:

> 'No way am I the one who can save people from themselves,' he told them. 'People, listen up! I'm just the warm-up act: the messenger. The real Messiah comes later, and he's much greater than me. I'm not even fit to tie his shoelaces. I'm happy to baptise you with water, but when the real power arrives on the scene, you'll not know what's hit you. He'll baptise you with the Holy Spirit. You'll feel it like a fire that completely changes you from the inside out.'

Comment:

It is a difficult thing to pass up on adulation and not revel in the generous accolades that people are sometimes willing to give us. We all like to be popular. The feel-good factor generates a satisfying internal glow.

John the Baptist voluntarily gives away the possibility of being self-important. He knows that if he presents himself as something he's not, they'll eventually rumble him and see through the veneer and facade. John refuses to take the glory and praise for himself.

Prayer:

We pray for those like John,
who are willing to humble themselves,
and pass up on the possibility of popularity

so that others may invest in real hope.
Some are voices crying in the wilderness,
others are those who are brave enough to take up unpopular causes.
Some speak for those who have no voice,
and others are those who, in modesty and humility,
point to a more profound,
fulfilling and satisfying way of being:
the way of goodness and Godness,
which leads to more wholesome living and eternal life.

Symbolic action (drinking the water):

So let us drink the water, a sign of John.
We do it to remember him,
and what he did to point folk God-ward.
And as we drink, let it be a sign
that we also will try to do the same in these Advent days.

All drink the water.

Mary

Responses:

Leader:	People of God, what do we wait for at this Advent time?
All:	We wait to receive the personal invitation of God.
Leader:	And why is this bottle of milk here?
All:	It stands for the young girl Mary: the one who, though hesitant at first, chose to accept God's unreasonable invitation.
Leader:	And what do we celebrate this Advent?
All:	We rejoice that, when the time was right, it was a hesitant and scared teenage girl who said 'Yes'; who agreed to host divinity within her own body,

and so harboured heaven's promise,
and nurtured justice and delivered freedom
for the whole human race.

Reading: Luke 1:26–38 (NRSV):

In the sixth month the angel Gabriel was sent by God to a town in Galilee called Nazareth, to a virgin engaged to a man whose name was Joseph, of the house of David. The virgin's name was Mary.

And he came to her and said, 'Greetings, favoured one! The Lord is with you.' But she was much perplexed by his words and pondered what sort of greeting this might be.

The angel said to her, 'Do not be afraid, Mary, for you have found favour with God. And now, you will conceive in your womb and bear a son, and you will name him Jesus. He will be great, and will be called the Son of the Most High, and the Lord God will give to him the throne of his ancestor David. He will reign over the house of Jacob for ever, and of his kingdom there will be no end.'

Mary said to the angel, 'How can this be, since I am a virgin?' The angel said to her, 'The Holy Spirit will come upon you, and the power of the Most High will overshadow you; therefore the child to be born will be holy; he will be called Son of God. And now, your relative Elizabeth in her old age has also conceived a son; and this is the sixth month for her who was said to be barren. For nothing will be impossible with God.'

Then Mary said, 'Here am I, the servant of the Lord; let it be with me according to your word.' Then the angel departed from her.[1]

Comment:

When all's said and done, it has to be acknowledged that she was the most unlikeliest of people: *'Not the foremost of her gender; not the finest of her race.*[2] And yet this slip of a girl is the one in whom God chooses to invest the entire future of the human race. The product of her womb, though she didn't know it at the time, was to change the world completely.

God entrusted the earth's destiny to an ordinary human being. God still entrusts the earth's destiny to ordinary human beings, like you and me. That's a scary thought. Because of what we know of other people and the damage they can do, and because of what we know of ourselves and the serious damage we can do, we might be forgiven for questioning God's wisdom in this particular matter. But that seems to be God's preferred method. Consistently this is the way God chooses to work.

As far as the destiny of this world and its people is concerned, what, then, is the particular responsibility each of us has been given? Mercifully, it may or may not be that we are to give birth to a baby – something that would be especially problematic for men! But some other responsibility might be allotted to each of us perhaps? Some other task that God may be asking us to do during these Advent days?

In the quietness, let's take a few moments to consider this. What could it be? In the quietness of this place we might also want to give our 'Yes' to God.

Time of reflection …

Prayer:

We pray for those who, like Mary,
have made a definite choice;
those who, despite their fears,
have deliberately given their 'Yes' to God.
We give thanks for the folk who gave us life,
and who nurtured us with encouragement – and criticism.
We give thanks for the folk around us today
who shape our opinions, and reform our character
and enable us to grow even more in love.

And, God, will you help us if we have said 'Yes!' to you?
And will you give us the strength and determination
to see the job through?

Symbolic action (drinking the milk):

We drink the milk:
a reminder of Mary who was prepared to do
what was asked of her.
It is a reminder too of mothers,
who give the very essence of themselves to the children they love;
a reminder too of fathers who, in their own way, do the same.
And as we drink,
let that be a sign of our intentions:
that we will try to be faithful
in carrying out the work of compassion and care
which God always asks his friends to undertake.

All drink the milk.

Jesus

Responses:

Leader:	People of God,
	what do we hope for in this Advent time?
All:	We hope for the Christ, promised by God.
Leader:	Why has this candle been lit?
All:	It is a sign of Jesus,
	the light who always shines in the darkness;
	the light that can never be put out.
Leader:	And why is this broken bottle here?
All:	It stands for the struggle
	between the time of birth and the time of death;
	the struggle of Jesus,
	the struggle that is ours,
	the struggle that is life.

Leader: People of God, here is the good news of God:
             Christ has come!
             Christ is here!
             Christ is coming!
All   The light of Christ to give direction.
             The light of Christ to shine in forgotten places.
             The light of Christ to bring healing.
             The light of Christ to give wholeness.
             The light of Christ to make peace for us all.

Reading: Luke 1:68–75 (GNB):

Let us praise the Lord, the God of Israel! He has come to the help of his people and has set them free. He has provided for us a mighty Saviour, a descendant of his servant David. He promised through his holy prophets long ago that he would save us from our enemies, from the power of all those who hate us. He said he would show mercy to our ancestors and remember his sacred covenant. With a solemn oath to our ancestor Abraham, he promised to rescue us from our enemies and allow us to serve him without fear, so that we might be holy and righteous before him all the days of our life.[3]

Comment:

'Christmas is a time for the children.' We hear that kind of remark often enough. But it is worth noting that he was the only child in that stable at Bethlehem: the rest of them were adults. In this serious business of the incarnation of himself, God meant serious business for adults. That means we cannot possibly keep this baby wrapped up in swaddling clothes, nor should we leave him lying all snug and cosy in a manger, warmed by the breath of animals. For as we know, soon – too soon – after the *'Sing lullaby'* came *'the cross, the nails, the piercing ... conquering death, its bondage breaking'.*[4]

Between the birth and the death was the light: the God-light; the Jesus-light; the revelation; the example; the demonstration of the Way; the complete turning upside down of accepted thinking and understanding and perceptions of God. Between the birth and the death, we see what it means to live as one of his followers and friends.

From the conscious choices we as individuals make in response to the God-light are born ideas, notions, impulses, and these can only be satisfied and fulfilled when they are translated into realistic practical action. This may well result in personal sacrifice, or moving from the comfortable to the risky unknown. It may mean that heads are required to be raised above parapets. It may mean personal sacrifice. It may involve the dismantling and removal of barriers which divide God's own people. But that was precisely the point of those difficult 33 years. It was certainly the reason for all the deliberate and courageous speaking out. It was why healthy, grown-up, adult, precious red blood was spilled.

We are God's light now, and the candle continues to burn – or not – depending on what we choose. God took a risk by investing in the human Mary: God continues to take risks by investing in you and me. It is through us that he expects there to be:

- controversy, where there is cosiness and contentedness in the face of injustice;

- disturbance and upset, where there is disrespect and apathy in the face of the prospect of peace;

- challenge, where there is callous couldn't-care-lessness in the face of cruelty and corruption;

- disruption, where danger is dumbed-down, and this earth and the well-being of God's precious people are put under threat.

The birth we look forward to is not only about angel voices sweetly singing, for the Incarnation is also about the internalised struggles that need to be fought; external arguments that need to be engaged in; tables that need to be thumped really hard. Christmas is not child's play, for God is serious about it and means real business.

During this Advent, let us keep in mind the candle flame. It represents each of us as individual people, for we also are the light of the world. Let us be determined to burn brightly and shine out clearly through the darkness: bright flames for God's sake, for our own sake, for the good of us all.

Symbolic action (drinking the wine):

We drink the blood-red wine,
a sign of Jesus who made the ultimate sacrifice;
a reminder of those who put the welfare and well-being of others
before their own.
And let it be a sign to ourselves
that, in these Advent days,
knowing full well that it may in some way cost us,
we will try, like John, to point others God-ward;
like Mary, to give what is needed of ourselves;
and like Jesus, to stand out as beacons
in the eternal cosmic battle
for justice and compassion and grace.

All drink the wine.

Notes and sources:

1. New Revised Standard Version Bible, copyright 1989, Division of Christian Education of the National Council of the Churches of Christ in the United States of America. Used by permission. All rights reserved.

2. From 'Justice in the womb', *Innkeepers & Light Sleepers: Seventeen New Songs for Christmas*, John L. Bell, Wild Goose Publications, www.ionabooks.com

3. From the Good News Bible © 1994 published by the Bible Societies/HarperCollins Publishers Ltd UK, Good News Bible © American Bible Society 1966, 1971, 1976, 1992. Used with permission.

4. From 'The infant King (Sing lullaby)', Basque carol, paraphrased by Sabine Baring-Gould

Here is a cross

A meditation for Advent

Jan Sutch Pickard

This can be used in an all-age act of worship, such as a carol service. Include different voices, and possibly a movement of people to a central part of the church while carrying a simple wooden cross.

Here is a cross –
a sign of the love
in the life of a man
who shows us the way that God loves.

Here is a woman
who said 'Yes' to God
and carried the baby
who grew to a man
and showed us the way that God loves.

Here's an old man,
who worked with his hands
and hammered the wood,
who cared for the woman
who carried the baby
who grew to a man
who showed us the way that God loves.

This is the landlord in Bethlehem town
who saw they had travelled a very long way
and lent them a shed with hay for a bed
where the old man who worked with his hands
cared for the woman
who gave birth to the baby
who grew to a man
who showed us the way that God loves.

These are the shepherds,
out in all weathers,
who heard the good news
and came running down
to Bethlehem town

to find in the shed the landlord had lent –
just an old man who worked with his hands
and cared for the woman
who carried her baby
who grew to a man
and showed us the way that God loves.

These are poor people
all sad and afraid
and ill and alone
who saw the Good News
in the life of the man
who showed us the way that God loves.

These are the children
who wanted to play –
more joyful than grown-ups
who chased them away –
and found they belonged
very close to the man
who showed us the way that God loves.

You are the people
to share the Good News
of the small children who came to belong,
and the poor people who found that they were free,
and the rough shepherds who glorified God,
and all busy people who find a small space –
for the old man who worked with his hands,
and the young woman who said 'Yes' to God,
and that baby boy
who grew to a man
and carried a cross
and shows us the way that God loves.

Christ in the time of strife

Mary's memories: narratives for the four weeks of Advent

Rosemary Power

Introduction

Today we are deeply conscious of the crisis faced by refugees from our wars – those fleeing from Syria, Afghanistan, Iraq and Pakistan; from oppression in Eritrea and the largely ignored wars of South Sudan, Congo and beyond; from the collapse of Zimbabwe and the terrors of northern Nigeria; and, far to the east, from genocide in Myanmar ...

In Europe we have been affected; but we, in this rich and relatively stable part of the world, have been divided. We are aware in Britain, as never before in our times, of the division between rich and poor and that the Benefits system is distorted against the poor, and our health system is crumbling for lack of funds.

This is the world in which we are called to preach the Prince of Peace. But what is a prince and what is peace? We explore this through the scriptures that are the Christian baseline in life.

The word 'Lord' comes from the Old English, meaning 'bread-provider'. This was the term for the warrior leader of a household, the local prince.

We know that Mary, the mother of Jesus, survived her son. In these narratives, we take the Gospel stories of the Nativity in a different order, seen through her memories: of Jesus lost; of the killings in Bethlehem, the 'House of Bread', and life on the road; of the offering of Jesus in the temple; and how the story started for her.

Week one: Temple times

Song:

'I wonder as I wander out under the sky'

Bible reading:

Luke 2:39–52

Mary reflects:

Sometimes it's easier to tell it the other way,
the last things first, the first last.
Of how we lost him and found him
and lost him again but kept looking
and found him again, for a time.

There were hard times
with a growing boy –
after the years, the tears –
the child with stars in his eyes
and flame lighting his heart in a wind
that rushed like a storm from the hills or flowed like a tide
and stilled with his loving, loving without smothering,
always there, shared, clear
and just that bit
ahead of where we were: the youth of today!
Seeking and sharing, and breaking our hearts as he learnt
this is how villages work and the big world as well.
Be gentle as God, but as wise, wise without years.

After all that had been:
all the miles, the wiles of mercenary men
who seeing us stretched, stretched us for refuge
in the desert of our hopes.
We snatched at small kindness – a cup of cold water –
on the predatory route

of refugees and strangers
the world over.
And we swore
we'd raise our child different,
with God's word in his ears,
a temple in his heart, from the start.
A place apart.

And then, when all seemed settled, he'd be off again
upon that father's business.

We'd brought him safe to the banquet of the poor
and there was no way back.
Jerusalem, our hope, made desert,
the shepherd followed the sheep
into that wilderness where
the wild beasts ravaged him
and angels watched.
Sometimes kindness says
stay away. I waited there all day.
And two days more. As ever.

We longed for Messiah to come with a sword and the power
to drive out oppressors, the greedy, the evil and vile,
and found a child willing to hold the earth's pain in his hands.

We'd prayed for a temple again and found
God had chosen our time and the cruel and the brave
and entered our world with a temple of flesh
where the veil would be torn and we'd meet face to fact.

We found him at last,
in the place where, years before,
we'd dedicated our firstborn.
He came back, mild as ever,
and grew in the workshop of his world.

Prayers:

We pray today for children tossed upon the world too young, children who miss the love that makes us strong to love and lose and learn again; for those who wandered and forgot to plot the way home. Creator, shelter your children this night: those in flight, those trapped in fighting, those delighting in freedom and those whose innocence is at risk.

Loving Creator, who made each one, wondrously, curiously, exceptionally, be with each one and bring them to where they may grow in wisdom and stature and the strength of love that will last.

We pray for the world's missing children. We pray for those who seek them. That the loyalty of love be requited.

We pray for the child who cries with no one to hear, the orphaned, bereaved, those with parents in prison or missing. We pray for children heading families, learning the skills and giving to siblings, at the cost of their own freedom to be young, of their education and dreams.

We pray for refugees on the road and sea, for those forced to live among strangers, for those who travel in terror of the night, among people-traffickers and smugglers and those who have lost the sense of the sacred. We pray for ourselves, that you unlock our freezing wealth and closed borders and hearts.

Open prayer for the needs of the young people of the world …

Lord's Prayer

Blessing:

May the Lord bless us and keep us;
the Lord make his face to shine upon us and be gracious unto us;
the Lord lift up his countenance upon us and give us peace.
Amen

Week two: The terror times

Song:

'Child in the manger, infant of Mary', original Gaelic by Màiri NicDhòmhnaill of Bunessan, translated by Lachlan Macbean

Bible reading:

Matthew 2:13–23

Mary reflects:

We got him back that time when he was young, back to the village and the gossip and the spite, and showed him how to live a different life. Though he was always ahead, he was always dutiful, always kind. With the kindness that killed him later. But first he had his trade, the years made, all but the girl who would warm the heart and the children we yearned for.

Like Moses he was wafted away to be great. Four centuries of silence found God not defeated by our deafness. Behind were those who didn't make it. We never went back to the House of Bread, to the place where our escape would hurt so deep in those who bore him no ill will, where they paid for their lifetimes the price for his life. Living among strangers, it took us years to hear what happened there. We slipped the mesh and took the road that saved us, away from our decoys from the east, down into Egypt. With the God of creation in my arms, helpless against pain.

In the terror times
the killing fields
came to the House of Bread.
How could those people forgive God
when the universe alive in each child was snapped, cast aside,
trampled as worthless.
Was there one solider that day, paid to slay,
who turned from his duty and passed by in silence to save?

We heard of Herod's lands and hands,
created in love by the God of creation,
of a man now in love with his greed
and the rage
that spoke to his soul in the cold.
While building the Temple of God he still killed
his sons, and the sons of the poor, the ones
Jesus had toddled with, eaten with, cried with and dozed
in the arms of their parents.

Only they and their God can forgive or withhold after wrong.
But can I forgive him the harm that he did to our years?

How can I pray for a man with a grave in his soul,
where the rotting is buried but wakes?
How can God carry a man who is slave
to his power and fear
and lust for the passing desires?

How can I feel for a soul in the cess of itself
who has lost the flame in his depth,
who is frightened to die while the skies shriek his deeds –
but created from love though distorted by self and its hate?

Yet what is forgiving but joining the soul to the Spirit,
El Shaddai of shadows, of silence alive
with the breath where all things may occur
in pain and quiet power at the cost of the love without end?

Prayers:

We pray for grace to forgive, through the act of will that joins us to the Spirit who suffers all with us.

We pray for grace to wait, not to speak, where forgiveness is for others to give.

We pray for those who cannot forgive. That one day they hold in their hands the knowledge that the past cannot be changed but is held by a God who will never cease to value and carry the cost.

We pray for all who suffer in war, for parents who cannot protect their young.

We pray for our world that loses the gifts that each person is called to bring.

We pray for those who survive, that they may be free of guilt for others who died and they could not save. We pray for those who witnessed, and we pray that those who abused the needs of the poor may turn back to God.

We pray for those who lost loved ones this year, in the bombings of *(name these)*. We pray for lands ruled by oppression and dictatorship *(name)* …

We pray for each person who stays their hand from power, for each act of charity and courtesy that saves and heals, that it be magnified and bear fruit one hundredfold.

Open prayer for those who are suffering …

Lord's Prayer

Blessing:

May the road rise behind us on our journey, the wind be at our back; may God be with us on the road and at the arrival. And may God be the guide, the light and the safety for all who journey this night. Amen

Week three: The House of Bread

Song:

'It came upon a midnight clear'

Reading:

Matthew 1:18–2:2

Mary reflects:

It wasn't what we'd hoped for:
Joseph's grand idea.

I was not liked by all but loved by some
at the village well.
Judgement was strong while I carried
peaceful dark in my womb.
Joseph knew grief but he said
leave all the gossip, the drip
born of small faith watered from shallow wells
tainted with pain from the common earth of our souls.
The village talked; we left
for the House of Bread,
where he'd got people
not counting the months
nor years, not then.

The doors seemed shut against us
as busy lives went on, with Joseph
doing casual work below the counter and his skills.
The Promise of Ages, of prophecy, coming
to give us our freedom, was silent.
So the birth came
as births come, then the temple and the cleansing and redemption.

That fortieth day we walked to Jerusalem
with country women with baskets

old men with olives
young men with passes
schoolgirls with dreams
delayed by the system but hoping
to walk home by nightfall.
A day's walk, a long road,
through every barrier we make
to reach the temple of the Lord.

It was a sight beyond our senses –
the noise and the swearing, buildings, construction and traffic,
armed soldiers in courts of the Gentiles, and women
and tradesmen and tourists and trampling.

Then, two old angels spoke –
Now let your servant go in peace
having seen our salvation –
and made us welcome.
My child was welcome in the courts of the Lord.
Two birds dropped from the wind, two blessings left
our sacrifice of sore feet
warmed with wisdom.
A light to enlighten the Gentiles
and give glory to your people, Israel.

Prayers:

We pray for all who find the wall on that road, an impediment to human witness.

We pray for the land where Jesus walked, that justice and peace may flourish.

We pray for those who joy in the birth of a child; and those who grieve like Rachel.

We pray for other divided places, the forgotten wars of Central Africa, for child soldiers with evil acts on stunted brains, and for their future.

We pray for the girls forced into encounters not of their will, for those kidnapped in Nigeria, Iraq, and those forced to work hidden in our own country.

We pray to hear the ache in the side of our God who created each one out of wonder, and found them returned to eternity before their time.

We pray for those who turn the world in their skilled hands. May they have the courage of Joseph, to dream the truth and waken to live it, at whatever the cost to themselves.

Open prayer for our journey into Advent and a deeper knowledge of God …

Lord's Prayer

Blessing:

Three slender strands that support the world:
the slender stream of milk into the pail,
the slender blade of corn in the ground,
the slender thread in the hand of a skilled woman.

Irish, 8th or 9th century

Week four: The answer

Song:

'The angel Gabriel from heaven came' (Medieval English, paraphrase by Sabine Baring-Gould)

Reading:

Luke 1:26–38, Matthew 1:18–25

Mary reflects:

Years later, when they told the story, and wrote it down for the Greeks overseas, when we knew of the other kingdom, they never said how Joseph saw the way God did it.

The day I met the messenger
who offered an answer
from the God of all courtesy who left
a lifetime to find the question
or walk away,
who gave me the one who asked questions
and prayed in the hills
and the one who dreamed questions
and paid the bills.

We waited centuries for Word
from the God who puts sin and refusal to use
and gave us the temple through Herod.

Why me? Why here? Had time lurched to a standstill:
a Messiah besmirched at birth
to lead us to victory?

To a God so generous I said yes.
And then remembered Joseph.

I speak of the good man who married me, went all the way with me. Who wanted shavings of wood for a lifetime, and a warm embrace in the evenings. Our village was tainted, and I was betrothed to a man who found work with the soldiers, and read from the scriptures and served the widows. Who threw up his trade and his father's house to follow a woman they called light as wind. The wind blew through his soul: it uprooted him. One night he left for us his life, his name, his family and friends for a future among strangers, or death on the road with a family he couldn't defend. He could have said: it is enough. I've done my duty to another's child. But he went with us down into Egypt and the workshop of the world.

He never said a word. Joseph in Egypt dreamed. The barns became full.

We'd waited so long for a Saviour. Then we learnt from a living temple. From his heart flowed streams of clear water. We learnt how prayer changes the world, and the word of the Lord can ease the heart of the stranger. That all are called to the banquet. That swords can be beaten to ploughshares. The question took a lifetime.

The love of my youth stayed with me and took me on journeys that stretched my heart to the edges.

A joiner before the dawn of time was to learn at his knee.

Prayers:

We pray for those faced with intractable questions, impossible demands. For those weighed down by work or fear.

For those in expectation, who find they are offered something different.

We pray for those who raise children, especially in times of strife, the carers and educators who seek to enlarge the mind of the child and help them find their place in the world.

We pray for children not fortunate in their parenting: may God grant them a white light in the back of their minds to guide them.

We pray for those in grief who see their child die before them. We pray for those who see their child take a wrong path through life.

We pray for peace, that the Lord of peace, the provider of bread and companions, may rule our lives and change the way we work the world. We name the places of our world that are hurting ...

Open prayer

Lord's Prayer

Blessing:

May God,
Creator, Redeemer, Sustainer,
bless us and keep us from all harm,
all wrongdoing,
and ever at the
service of our neighbour.
Amen

For contemplation:

'The Annunciation' by Edwin Muir and the *The Annunciation* by Fra Angelico

Readings for
Holocaust Memorial Day

Various contributors

Yitzchak Zieman (1920–2007):
from persecution to reconciliation

I got to know Yitzchak in 1977 in a workshop called 'Crisis in groups and individual crisis'. Later, we co-led workshops. When I visited him in New York, and later, in 2000 when he stayed with us – while giving some very moving talks to my congregation – he told me his life story:

In 1920, Lithuania was a small independent country. People got along well. Among Christians of different denominations and Jews there seemed to be tolerance and no discrimination. In the villages people lived together peacefully. Children went to the same schools and neighbours helped one another.

Yitzchak was the eldest of six children. In 1939, he joined the army to fight the Nazis. When they occupied his country, he got the sudden urge to go home to his village. But on the way he met a woman he knew: 'Don't go home,' she said. 'The villagers are killing all the Jews … All of your family are dead. And they will kill you too.' Yitzchak was shocked. Even his little sister had been killed?

He fled to Russia to fight the Germans, but as a Jew had no chance. He was arrested and sent to a gulag, where he nearly died of hunger. A young female doctor saved him. She managed to keep him in the infirmary until he was better and then helped him to escape.

His next memory was of being in a small town – and the smell of freshly baked bread. He walked into a bakery, and was handed a piece of bread. Then, suddenly, he turned, and saw a beautiful young woman, and so 'started to become a person again': a young man who was alive.

He travelled to Greece, where, again, he fought the Nazis. By the end of the war he was in hiding in Poland.

In May 1945, he came to Munich, where the American Occupation Services engaged him to work with Jews who had survived the concentration camps, as he spoke many languages. He had to listen to many terrible experiences. The task was too hard. After some time he ended up in a clinic.

When he recovered, he made the decision to become a psychotherapist – to be able to work with individuals who had been through the worst experiences – and obtained a visa to study in America.

In the U.S. he met other survivors of the Holocaust, like Ruth Cohn from Berlin. Together they developed a new way of working with groups called Theme-centred Interaction (TCI), to aid in better understanding, e.g. between black and white Americans, or different tribes and clans – a terrible mass killing like the Holocaust should never happen again.

In 1970, Ruth came back to Europe, bringing Yitzchak and other psychotherapists with her to help lead workshops and conferences. Yitzchak himself began to work on the theme: 'Jews and the children of the Nazis: what do we have to share which will help us to understand each other better?'

In 1980 he married, a German woman; and travelled to Israel as part of the 'Peace Now' movement. He wanted to work with Israelis and Palestinians, but was not welcome in the country. This must have been a very difficult experience for him as he did not want to talk about it.

What impressed me most about Yitzchak was his modesty when he spoke about his life, and his eagerness to listen to the experiences of others, especially Germans. Very late in life he was again able to sing the Yiddish songs from his childhood, part of a culture nearly extinguished by the Nazis.

I learned of Yitzchak's death when I was volunteering as an Ecumenical Accompanier in Palestine and Israel. His personality has encouraged me never to give up hope and to continue networking for peace and reconciliation.

Elisabeth Christa Miescher

It snowed again on Auschwitz

Pupils and staff of Silcoates School visited Auschwitz-Birkenau in March 2015, as part of the programme 'Lessons from Auschwitz' organised by the Holocaust Educational Trust (www.het.org.uk). In the following readings young people speak of the experience ... Finding the words is difficult ...

It snowed again on Auschwitz;
a thick white blanket
covering a million unmarked graves.
The familiar train-tracks
stretch on into the distance.
May our commitment
extend beyond this horizon,
beyond the memories
of a few numbered survivors
as we focus on the living
and never forget the dead.

Janet Lees, Chaplain, and the young people at Silcoates School

The suitcase

The suitcase was small.
It had a name on it
and an address.
It had belonged to someone.
Now it was piled up
in a mountain of others,
each with a different name.
Remember the dead
but do not forget the living.

Janet Lees, Chaplain, and the young people at Silcoates School

Remembering the Holocaust

When you go there
in person,
in the snow and biting wind,
and you see the buildings around you,
entering each one in turn
to be reminded of some further atrocity –
suitcases, glasses, hair, limbs –
even though you know about it,
even though you read a book,
or someone told you,
it's a struggle to take it in.

When you go there
into the place
that was a gas chamber
but now looks like an underground car park,
and you listen to the description,
or you see the ruined sites
that were the other crematoria,
blown up so as to conceal the truth,
you wonder about life and death,
about remembering and forgetting.

When you go there
and see the rails
where the wagons stood,
where the people were separated,
some for death
and some for death later,
and you recall the words of prophets
and of Christ himself,
you know that it is all you can do:
'You are my witnesses.'*

Janet Lees

* From the Gospel of John and the Book of Isaiah

The boy in the striped pyjamas*

I was the one who was there.
I was the one who went through it,
but you're only hearing my story here today.

What kind of bloody animals were they anyway?
For God's sake, I was only nine years old after all.
And if you're shocked, or insulted,
or offended by my language,
then to tell you the truth, I really don't care.
For there are worse things
that can happen to you in this life
than to listen to a child when he swears.

What kind of bloody animals were they?
They were fathers of pretty little girls,
mothers' sons, favourite uncles,
doting husbands, family men,
upright and respectable members
of their own communities.

Often they had sat by the fireside
and contentedly watched their own children play.
They had patted babies' backs,
tickled babies' chins,
rocked infants gently;
the kind of men who found their pleasure
in making little ones laugh.

They had looked on with pride
as they watched daughters blossom
and grow into maturity.
They had congratulated sons,
and encouraged them
with an enthusiastic: 'Well done!'
But, my God!
What kind of bloody animals were they?

How could they transform so dramatically?
How could they become such monsters?
How could they change, and become so different,
and turn into such subhuman beasts?

They made us wear flimsy, striped pyjamas,
tattooed numbers on our arms
and gave us hardly anything to eat.
In freezing temperatures we shook and shivered.
They made us slaves,
they made us suffer,
they turned us into feral creatures: jungle animals.
And if anyone became sick,
they were taken away
and made to disappear.

For idle amusement of an evening
they would set their dogs on us,
and then laugh.
A baby's arm was ripped open,
an old woman's face removed,
a teenager's leg lacerated from groin to knee.
You've no idea the damage that can be done
by snarling, vicious teeth.

And then, just for the fun of it,
the lashings and the beatings.
No excuse needed:
a soldier's amusement,
a jailer's prerogative:
another prisoner dead.
Thick black smoke rose daily.
There was nowhere to escape;
nowhere to avoid the sickening stench
and the nauseating smell.
It clung in the air,
it lived in your nostrils,
it was always with you.

We knew what was happening;
we knew what it meant …

What kind of bloody animals were they anyway?
I've thought about it a lot,
but can't come up with an answer.
I was only nine years old after all.
But one thing I do know for certain:
once upon a time those men were ordinary folk.
Maybe they just got corrupted by the fact of war;
got caught up in the purest kind of evil
that war always breeds.

And if you're shocked, or insulted,
or offended by my language,
then to tell you the truth,
on this Sunday morning,
I really don't care.
For there are many worse things
that can happen in this life
than to listen to a child when he swears.

Glendon Macaulay

* Inspired by the film *The Boy in the Striped Pyjamas*

Odd shoes

As part of our orientation to the complex situation in Israel/ Palestine, the Ecumenical Accompaniment team of which I was a part (www.eappi.org) visited Yad Vashem. The Holocaust Museum has a poignant pile of abandoned shoes. I remembered these, as I walked down to the barbed wire of the Security Barrier, and saw a single shoe lying at the roadside …

There's always a single shoe –
on the tideline among the wrack,
or at the roadside, in the white dust –

perished leather, no laces, scuffed,
holes in its sole;
but it has a tongue:
what story could it tell?

> I took off my shoes
> – at the door of your home
> – where you worship
> – to walk on your land.
> I am watching where I tread:
> I am not worthy
> to be such a welcome guest.

In your shoes,
so well-worn,
so kindly lent –
what can I do?

> New shoes for a holiday,
> skipping in the dust;
> worn with the joy
> of being young and fully alive –
> not yet worn down.

So many shoes:
left behind
when, one by one,
alone and together,
you took that last step.

Jan Sutch Pickard

Belsen picture

Her mouth is open
in a silent shout.
Their mouths are all open:
for she is on top of a pile
of bodies tossed together –
too many to count.

But they do count:
each once a person with a name.

They are shouting to us
but we cannot hear
what they are saying,
or imagine
what scenes they witnessed,
what despair felt, what pain
brought them to this place.

There is a terrible repose
in their starved and stripped limbs
and at the same time
such an urgency in their faces –
their open mouths shouting to us
across the years.

And we both shrink away,
and strain to catch the words:
'Never again …'
          … Never again?

Jan Sutch Pickard

How vibrant is the city: a prayer in praise of multiculturalism

How vibrant is the city –
alive at work and play.
The streets and parks echo
with voices in many languages.
Shops and businesses reflect
their worldwide roots and origins.
Our coming together
in council chamber and school,
hospital and factory
releases energy that expands
into the corners of every home.
How vibrant is the city!
Help us dream your dreams, God of all.
May your vibrant city arise
from this crucible of talent and commitment.

Janet Lees

Sources:

'Yitzchak Zieman (1920–2007): from persecution to reconciliation', by Elisabeth Christa Miescher, from *We Will Seek Peace and Pursue It: Reflections and prayers for peace and reconciliation*, Neil Paynter (Ed.), Wild Goose Publications, 2015

'It snowed again on Auschwitz', 'The suitcase', 'Remembering the Holocaust', 'How vibrant is the city: a prayer in praise of multiculturalism' © Janet Lees

'The boy in the striped pyjamas', from *Dirt, Mess and Danger: Liturgies & worship resources*, Glendon Macaulay, Wild Goose Publications, 2011

'Belsen picture' and 'Odd shoes', by Jan Sutch Pickard, from *Between High and Low Water: Sojourner Songs*, Wild Goose Publications, 2008

Prayers for lighting candles

Ruth Burgess

Introduction

These prayers could be used in a daily discipline by an individual or a group over a period of days or weeks.

The prayers were originally written for two City of London churches which are open daily for visitors. The churches have stands of votive candles and wanted some prayers that could be used by folk lighting them.

The prayers could be made into a leaflet or printed onto individual prayer cards, possibly with an illustration. Some of the prayers are written for individuals to use as petitions, intentions or thanksgivings. Some are intercessory prayers and blessings for others.

Starmaker God,
Lightener of the world,
bless us and warm us
into light and loving.
Bring us to
the light of Jesus
all the length and breadth
of our nights and days.

As the candle
so my life:
flickering, burning, changing,
alight and warm
with the light
which is You.

Candle flames
dance.
They are beautiful.
They give us light.
They warm us.

Let this candle
be a sign
that I have
asked You
to dance,
and burn,
and shine
in me.

In this still place
the candle flame
burns.
When I breathe
and blow on it
it dances.

Breathe in me,
Holy Spirit:
blow away my hesitation.
I want to dance with You.

You love me.
You are my Maker.
You know me.
You dance in and out
of my footsteps.
God, Light of the universe,
shine in me.

You love me.
You are my friend.
You know me.
You challenge my darkness.
Jesus, Light of the streets
around me,
shine in me.

You love me.
You hug me.
You are closer to me
than breathing.
You give me hope and courage.
Holy Spirit, Light of my journey,
shine in me.

I light a candle.
A sign that
I know
that God loves me.

I light a candle.
A sign that
I want to walk
with Jesus today.

I light a candle.
A sign that
I want the Holy Spirit
to breathe in me.

I light a candle
and I ask that
God's love
and God's glory
may shine through me.

As a candle burns
giving warmth and light,
so may I live
a warm
truthful
loving
and
hopeful
life.

God of the universe,
You made light
in the darkness.

I have lit a candle.

God of the universe,
You make my darkness light.

Thank You.

Jesus,
I want to walk with You.
Shine in my darkness.
Circle me with truth and loving.
Come and share in my tears and laughter.
Help me to be just and courageous.
I want to walk in Your light.

Jesus,
You called me to love and share,
to shine for You.

I sometimes flicker,
sometimes get blown out.
When this happens
come, through friends and strangers,
come and love me.
Come and re-light my candle,
my flame, my hope,
my love, my joy.

A candle burns.
A flame dances.
Burn away the darkness in me.
Fill me with warmth
and truth
and light.

God
I have got
used to the darkness.
Something in me
is afraid of
Your love and light.

As I light
this candle
remind me
that You
are warm
and loving,
that You call me
to live in Your light.

As I leave
this candle burning
I leave *(name)*
in Your warmth
and in Your light.
Look after *(name)*, God.

Lighting a candle
is an act of defiance.

Lighting a candle
is a prayer for courage.

Lighting a candle
is a step towards God.

Out in the world,
where You are
and I live,
help me today
to light a candle,
a candle of love and life.

God of light.
Be with those
who are in dark places.
Be with those
who are hungry or hurting.
Be with those who are in danger.
Be with those who today will die.
As I light this candle
kindle the flame of Your love in me.

Let me shine:
where You send me,
where people need me,
where You cry.

Sun, moon and stars.
A small candle.
All these
bring light
dancing.

And so can you.

May God bless you
and shine in you

all the nights and days
of your journey home.

A candle for *(name)*.
A candle for my friends
and family *(names)*.
A candle for my hopes and dreams …

I light a candle.

As it burns
may my prayers
be heard
by God.

Amen

You love me.
You call me
to share my resources
and work for justice,
to laugh and cry with strangers
and neighbours.
You call me to be light.

All this, God.
It's enormous!

All I can do is light a small flame,
a tiny candle …
And You take it and laugh
and bless it.
You use it to shine Your wonder

and warmth and joy
through the world,
through the universe,
through me.

Credo:
I love You.
You're amazing.

God,
wherever You lead me,
I will walk with You.

Love has many faces

A meditative prayer
for Valentine's Day

Ian M Fraser

Lord God – you fairly take our breath away!

We give thanks for the adventurous way you choose to relate to your creation, giving freedom and instilling a flair for initiative in all creatures, so that, for instance, over aeons of time, Galapagos finches chose to hone their beaks to suit the food they favoured.

We give special thanks for the way you formed humanity, bearing a family likeness to yourself, and risking your choice of us – well-knowing the good and bad in our natures – to share with you the work of bringing the world to its true fulfilment. What is more, when we let you down, your covenant with us stays firm and sure – because you, the one who fashioned us for freedom, have kept faith in us against the odds.

We give great thanks that you did not play safe in appointing the manner of our creation. We could have been fashioned as flower bulbs are, multiplying offspring by accretion. You had better things in store for us. You chose to make us sexual beings – well-knowing that our sexual natures comprised combustible material capable of engendering good or evil behaviour. You did not hold back. You wanted us to relish the delights of sexuality, and be willing to take its risks in our stride. Succeeding generations are thus entrusted with a dangerous freedom by you. Male and female are blessed together. You counselled us:

> *'Away you go and get on with life. Use your inbred initiatives, beget successors and spread over the earth. Take charge, sharing in my work of transforming the earth, eradicating wrong growth here, encouraging good development there, acting as my trustees and stewards'* (Genesis 1:27–28, 2:15).

We stand in awe before the venturing in love which you have undertaken and continue to undertake for our sakes, your power made the servant of your grace.

So we can give thanks for a world marked by *'your goodness at the heart of humanity, planted more deeply than all that is wrong'* (Iona Community affirmation).

We rejoice that there are those of different sex who find they are made for one another and covenant to live together in love; who can welcome one another into bodily union, searching one another out delightfully ... till, in a crescendo of delirious abandonment, they pour their beings into one another in joyous self-giving unity.

We bless you for times of more quietly expressed self-giving love, not reaching the heights but quietly, warmly affirming one another in an affection which carries couples through the ups and downs of daily life and gives life relish; also for occasions of awkwardness, at times when readiness of partners fails to converge, and the union is confirmed and sealed by the thoughtfulness and sensitive understanding shown, the depth of mutual commitment made secure by surviving all kinds of circumstances.

We rejoice in those who, through choice or 'in the run of the play', experience no such bond but enlarge life for themselves and others as good friends and neighbours, expressing a different fullness of being which enriches their community.

We give thanks for those who find depth of sustaining relationship in a member of their own sex, given that gift according to the way they were created, and using it to express the wideness of God's grace – as, in his time, King David mourned the death of his friend Jonathan: '*Your love to me was wonderful, passing the love of women*' (2 Samuel 1:26). And for those of mixed gender who may need your sustaining love for them to be expressed by us in friendship.

We pray for those let down by what they thought was love and proved to be barren, that your grace may prove to be sufficient for them, and that those who look to you may affirm them and help them through difficult times.

In all this we ask your grace for those in a situation of courtship, sussing out a relationship, trying to find whether mutual attraction and friendship reveal the existence of deeper roots which can lead to depth of commitment to share a unity of life.

Lead them, we pray, to whatever provides fulfilment for themselves and others.

You, God of love, whose Son walked on water, guide those who dice with the future to a life of grace and love, whatever the character of their relationship; that your risk-taking with us may prove to be justified and our sensitiveness to one another play its part in the coming of your kingdom and the doing of your will on earth as in heaven.

Sending Valentine cards:

To make St Valentine's Day special, with a recognition of the many faces of love which life allows for, send:

- *a special card to the one who means more to you than life itself*

- *another ordinary greeting, well-wishing card to someone who may be neglected, recognising that God's love has no boundaries.*

A Lenten and Easter cycle

Thom M Shuman

Ash Wednesday

Ashes, ashes ...

Burning your covenant
behind me,
I race on ahead
to jump on this
weary-go-round
called life,

sin spinning me
faster and faster,
until I fall off,
dizzily dancing with
death.

Getting ready for bed,
I bank the embers
of my ever-faithful fears,
hoping they might
smoulder into cold cinders
I can scatter
to the Spirit;

in the morning, I hurriedly
splash my face
with a few handfuls
of the leftover ashes
from yesterday's
feast on foolishness;
ashes, ashes,
we all fall down ...

into the embrace
of your grace.

First Sunday of Lent

Like a kitten

My temptations do not come
like a prowling lion
seeking to devour me;
no:
like a kitten,
they curl up in my lap
purring me to complacency.

My desert experience
is not somewhere
'out there' –
it is shuffling papers
at my desk;
dumping another load
of dirty jeans
into the machine;
commuting in my car,
listening to my angry voice
at the drivers around me
echo the ones on the radio.
The Evil One
is too smart to come to me
in a halloween costume
but comes
in the neighbour
a couple of doors down
who fears the way life is changing;
in the knot of teenagers
walking down the street towards me;
in any person, in every person,
who is not my child, my spouse, me.

Tempted One:
strengthen me with your word,

feed me with the sweetness of your grace,
shelter me in the coolness of your love;
then, together,
we can journey to Jerusalem.

Second Sunday of Lent

Names

Traducer
seducer
accuser
persecutor:
all those people I can be
when I follow
the wrong profit;

rebuker
quibbler
nitpicker
hair-splitter:
of all the faults
I spot so easily
in those around me;

croaker
complainer
grumbler
mumbler:
every time my life doesn't go
exactly as I asked God
to create it;

bellyacher
whiner
murmurer
moaner:

when everyone acts
as if it isn't all about
me.

I've met the enemy
and he is behind me,
pushing me
further and further

from you.

Third Sunday of Lent

Decalogue

We kept scuffing out
those ten words with
our shifty lives:

crossing the boundary
of a vowed relationship;

taking the breath away
from one of your
children;

leaning over the backyard
fence
to sow weeds
in a friend's
heart …

So we would not
keep thinking we
were so wise,

you took
a piece of wood
and

drew a line
in our souls

which death,
disappointment,
chaos
can never erase.

Fourth Sunday of Lent

Snakebit

Slowly,
so leisurely
I do not take notice,
the dullness of sin
wraps itself about
my fluttering hopes
(until I can no longer
see my soul
in front of me);
slyly,

whispering comforting
words of emptiness,
my murmurs of discontent
meander through my heart
until they become
the only voice
I trust;

sinuously,
with a wink,
a turn of the head,
a flicker of its tongue,
success wends its way
around my faith
squeezing tighter and tighter

until I have no breath
left
to offer praises.

But with the sharp point
of a nail,
you excise my wounds,
anointing them with grace,
wrapping them in
the balm of your
love.

Fifth Sunday of Lent

Wishing

I wish to see Jesus:
in the panhandler on Main Street –
but the unkempt hair,
the stained, tattered clothes,
the odours fit for a barnyard
cloud my eyes;

I wish to hear Jesus:
in the politicians
making decisions I cannot support;
in the evangelist
mouthing platitudes to the pain-full;
in the talk-show callers
spewing hateful bile;
but their words
clog my ears;

I wish to meet Jesus:
in the tattooed skateboarder
riding the rails at the school;
in the hip-hopper
jamming at the bus stop;

in the goths hanging outside
the video arcade,
but too quickly I cross the street
looking for him in folk
just like me.

Jesus:
why would you wish
to see
to hear
to meet
me?

Sixth Sunday of Lent: Palm/Passion Sunday

But later …

Joy dances down
the street,
grabbing us by the hand,
twirling us round
and round
as glad tears and songs
make a carpet
of welcome
for the one who comes.

But later …
we'll strip the branches
to weave
a cross;
stones that echoed
'Hosanna!'
will bloody the knees
of the stumbling
servant;

we'll dust off
our cloaks
and swaddle ourselves
to ward off
the cold breath
of death
sweeping down
from the Skull.

And when we
look back at everything
we could have
done
it will be
too late.

Holy Monday

*Mary took a pound of costly perfume made of
pure nard, anointed Jesus' feet, and wiped them
with her hair. The house was filled with the
fragrance of the perfume.* (John 12:3, NRSV)

Because

Because
we have preserved our grace
in manna jars
for the long winter of despair,
storing them in the dark corners
of our souls,
we have forgotten
its gritty taste;

because
we have put a tight lid
on our joy,

and put it in the back
of the pantry,
we have forgotten
how it can tickle
our noses;

because
we are so busy
prattling pious platitudes
about the poor, the least, the lost,
we ignore your words
which anoint them
as your children;

because
we have put up
the shutters and storm doors
to keep your future
from sneaking in,
we have missed
the sweet breeze
carrying your hope
to us;

because
we are who we are,
restore us, Holy Grace,
and make us
a fragrant offering to the world.

Holy Tuesday

Now among those who went up to worship at the festival were some Greeks. They came to Philip, who was from Bethsaida in Galilee, and said to him, 'Sir, we wish to see Jesus.' (John 12:20–21, NRSV)

Our eyes

Our eyes
easily slide past the
dishevelled, hollow-eyed
fellow with the
hand-printed sign:
'Wounded veteran cannot find work
have mercy on me';

our eyes
constantly
flickering to
our car's touchscreen,
we do not
notice the old woman
bundled in three
coats on a
summer's day,
pushing her cart
with her life piled
high in it;

our eyes
glued to our
handheld device
while dragging
our dog on the
early-morning
walk, we miss

the kids on the
corner
selling baked goods
for a classmate's
chemo costs;

we could see you,
Jesus,
but we are
usually looking
the other way.

Holy Wednesday

After saying this Jesus was troubled in spirit, and declared, 'Very truly, I tell you, one of you will betray me' … When he had gone out, Jesus said, 'Now the Son of Man has been glorified, and God has been glorified in him. If God has been glorified in him, God will also glorify him in himself and will glorify him at once.' (John 13:21, 31–32, NRSV)

Kitchen whispers

Taking the tray
from the server,
she slides the dirty
dishes
into the warm, soapy
water;

turning,
she grabs the pots
and pans,
banging them as
loudly
as she can, muttering

(not so softly)
to herself, 'There he
goes again,
talking in riddles
that no one can
solve. Why
can't he just come
out and say
things plainly?'

Turning from
the door where
she is eavesdropping,
Mary hushes, 'Quiet,
sister! I think
this may be
important.'

Holy Thursday

*Jesus, knowing that the Father had given all
things into his hands, and that he had come
from God and was going to God, got up from
the table, took off his outer robe, and tied a
towel around himself. Then he poured water
into a basin and began to wash the disciples'
feet and to wipe them with the towel that was
tied around him. He came to Simon Peter, who
said to him, 'Lord, are you going to wash my
feet?' Jesus answered, 'You do not know now
what I am doing, but later you will understand.'*
(John 13:3–7, NRSV)

Uncomfortable ...

... that's how we
feel, when

the basin of
water is
set before us,
the gentle ripples
of your love
caressing the
surface of that
life
of service
to which you
call us,

yet
we cannot bring
ourselves
to even dip
just our toes
in;

and it won't
be
until tomorrow
that we realise
what you are
really doing
is
showing us
you
will never,
ever,
wash your hands
of
us.

Holy Friday

Excarnation

A mother
once again cradles
her son, swaddling
him in
soft garments woven
from her grief;

shepherds stand gazing
from a nearby
hillside,
weeping at all
they had seen and
heard;

myrrh is taken from
the back shelf
where it has
gathered dust
through all the
years;

and angels
weep
silently
as
Jesus
returns home
by
another
road.

Holy Saturday

The dustman

Pushing his wheeled
bin before him,
the trash collector
goes on his early-
morning rounds

throwing a handful
of bent, bloodied
nails
onto the piles of
dreams turned
to ashes;

bundling up
the splintered
crossbeam
cast aside after
the latest
execution;

gathering
the empty wine
bottles, the cup and die
the soldiers left
behind
at the graveyard;
and tossing a
cracked board
which reads
'King of the Jews'
in three languages
on top of all
the other
fragments of
faith,

he trundles down
the hill into
misty
silence.

Easter Day

Early

Early in the morning
you put the brightly
coloured eggs and
chocolate goodies
in all the baskets piled
high with plastic grass,
giving them to the E.B.
to deliver while you
went back to bed ...

(no?)

early in the morning
you put on your
invisibility cloak and,
after stupefying
the guards, you
waved your wand,
rolling the stone
away ...

(no?)

early in the morning
Jesus felt around
the floor of the
tomb,
until he found

the bag in the corner,
and pulling on the
tights, as well as the shirt
with the big red S,
he broke the stone
into a million pieces,
and flew off, his cape
flapping in the wind …

(still no?)

OK then, how about?:

very
early in the morning
when our fears were
still in their cups,
you sat in the darkness,
cradling your silenced
Word,
as your tears
carved rivers through
chaos, and your
voice cracked with anguish
as you whispered:

'Let there be life'

and

he is.

Source:

Passages from NRSV copyright 1989, Division of Christian Education of the National Council of the Churches of Christ in the United States of America. Used by permission. All rights reserved.

Come dancing

A Bible study and reflection for Lent

Ian M Fraser

Lent has traditionally been marked by self-discipline, of which fasting is a sign.

When Margaret and I ministered in Rosyth, in Scotland, the Kirk Session came to the point where we started every meeting with an hour of Bible resourcing. On one occasion we fastened on the Mount of Transfiguration scene and what followed (Mark 9:14–29, e.g. ISV). When the disciples asked why they could not heal the epileptic boy whose father called for help, Jesus is said to have answered that the lad could not be cured except by prayer and fasting. The session wondered if we were missing out on an obligation to fast. We agreed on a Bible-search to see if, at some other point, light might be shed for us. We homed in on Isaiah 58, which we found enlighten-ing. The prophet lambastes those who make a big deal of fasting in public, while their conduct to others is abominable: *'Look, you serve your own inter-est on your fast day and oppress all your workers'* (Isaiah 58:3, NRSV).

Fasting is nothing in itself. Isaiah goes on (from verse 6) to indicate the kind of fasting which God looks for: *'… to loose the bonds of injustice, to undo the thongs of the yoke, to let the oppressed go free and to break every yoke … to share your bread with the hungry, and bring the homeless poor into your house …'*

If fasting is practised which is all show that is damnable. It should lead to just and compassionate relationships with others, especially the poor.

Lent has been observed from early times as a preparation for Easter. From earliest days fasting has been commended in certain Churches as an appro-priate part of that preparation. But does faith require fasting?

When the scriptures were copied by hand, it was possible for an ascetic copier to add a couple of words to indicate what might be regarded as implicated in the text. In the case of the Mount of Transfiguration there are reliable alternative, ancient texts which give Jesus' words simply as: *'This kind can come out only by prayer.'*

It is not quite but almost certain that Jesus and his disciples did not fast. See Mark 2:18–20: *'Why do John Baptist's disciples fast … but your disciples do not fast?'* Jesus said to them: *'The wedding guests cannot fast while the bride-*

groom is with them ... The days will come when the bridegroom is taken away from them, and then they will fast ...' Fasting is spoken of not as a deliberately chosen self-discipline but as a natural reaction in a time of loss, and then applies only up to the Resurrection, when 'the bridegroom' returns.

The Oxford Dictionary mentions the phrase having 'Lenten face', i.e. 'dismal'. Jesus uses the word translated as 'dismal' (*skuthropos*) in rebuttal in Matthew 6:16: *'Whenever you fast, do not look dismal, like the hypocrites, for they disfigure their faces as to show others that they are fasting.'* Fasting is a legitimate choice as long as it finds expression in daily commitments and is not for show. The scriptures do not treat it as a required commitment. We have to work out what comes into effective preparation for Easter.

Lent is meant to be a time when we develop our thinking and conduct by reflecting on the forty days and nights which Jesus spent in the wilderness in preparation for his mission. It chimes in with the understanding of fasting we find in the Isaiah 58 passage. Fasting God's way is not *'to bow down the head like a bulrush, and to lie in sackcloth and ashes'*. Jesus' fasting had a purpose to it – to sort out priorities for his mission.

Change stones into bread? An attractive possibility for one who was famished by fasting! But one for gaining populist kudos and distracting people from every word that comes from the mouth of God, the truly nourishing diet for all.

Float down from the pinnacle of the temple? A useless act, liable to flout the Father's genuine care, presenting that care as a bit of gimmickry, as magic.

Fall down and worship the Tempter? Material power was there for the taking – even in the last days twelve legions of angels, who could have wiped opposition off the face of the earth, were confined to barracks.

Jesus kept faith. The Father only was to be worshipped. He was the Father's man.

So today, whether or not we fast, how may we prepare for Easter?

I see a significant sign in the television programme *Strictly Come Dancing*. The merest amateurs, some who had not danced before in their lives, engage with professionals over a period. They can make amazing progress! In preparation for Easter, we can engage with this or that person in the Communion of Saints to learn better-furnished footwork of faith, freshly honed and matured. In such company we may be better able to take to the floor with the resurrected Christ at Easter and find unbelievable fulfilment.

It need not be one – it could be several saints over the weeks. They will need to be real biblical saints: not spiritual high achievers, but run-of-the-mill punters, ordinary people. Saints are not Church-appointed but Spirit-anointed. If I think of examples, I consider that top in God's eyes might be such as a wee wifie down a close who takes in two abandoned bairns and looks after them lovingly, or a binman who keeps the streets clean and recycles useful throwouts. The latter is illustrated in Ecclesiasticus 38. Doctors and intellectuals having been given due appreciation, the question is raised *'who sustains the fabric of the world?'*, i.e. keeps it going from day to day. Basic workers! *'All these put their trust in their hands … a town could not be built without them, there would be no settling or travelling … They give solidity to the created world … and their work-offering is in itself a form of prayer.'*

An Irish tradition pictures the Trinity not as static but as dancing in a circle – inviting all to join in the dance of life. Have a good dancing Lent!

Prayer

*May our life in community reflect
the dance of the Trinity,
by which the world is blessed.*

Iona Abbey Worship Book

Mothering God

Reflections for Mothering Sunday

Ruth Harvey

Who are we, as we stand before God, Mother-Father?

In the face of the love, activity and justice of our creator God, we stand naked. We stand both as givers of life, and as wrestlers for justice. We bring to birth life, and we seek right where life is denied in our world. In these reflections I acknowledge the influence and wisdom of feminist theologians such as Sallie McFague, who opened up new 'models of God' to me in her book of that title.

As the mother of three girls, I seek out those glimpses of God which volunteer themselves freely from their glory.

Dancing with angels

Child –
you are a burning bush.
Resting my eyes on you I see God
and the angels
swirling
whirling in around you.

Girl –
you are a still small voice.
In your gentler pace
in your 'Go slower, Mummy'
I hear the sound of God
(and the angels)
listening
in the spaces between us.

Babe –
your footsteps are holy ground.
Angels sing from your eyes, your lips,
through your giggle,
in your gentle sleeping breath.
In my rushing,
I lose eye contact,
I dance a different dance.

You are the sacred ground of being.
Let us touch, skin to skin –
me, stripped naked of my mask
of busyness,
open rather
to the rawness of God
embodied
in my body,
in your flesh,
in all creation through all of us.

So let us dance an angel dance together,
and meet God, face to face.

*This next poem was written at a time of intense peace talks
between the Palestinians and the Israelis. The agony and
exile of many millions of people sitting alongside the passion
on all sides to lay claim to a land, a story, which ultimately
unites rather than divides, struck me as universally poignant.
All creation is crafted from the universal love that is God-
creator, God Mother-Father. In our world religions we play
out, in horrific violence, our claim to Truth at the expense of
all others. This bold claim is one re-enacted on every parent's
lap, to which more than one child can lay an inalienable
claim. Are there lessons for us to learn here?*

Disputed territory

Two peoples, two histories:
One land, one story, bearing
the battle scars of the struggle.
Enemies, yet friends sitting
side by side – both staking
their equal and inalienable right
to the soil.

Two little girls, two histories:
One lap, one mother's body –

space each wants to occupy
wholly;
to which each has
her equal
and inalienable right.

No road map here will resolve
the unresolvable.
Only a heartfelt resolution
to love;
and to learn again,
as a child,
to share.

*The energy it takes to push a wholly separate creation out of
the mother's body is immense. The cord that unites mother
to child is a cord that both releases the one from other, and
at the same time unites the one with the other. The moment
of breaking the cord, of separation, is essential for life, but is
also painful. The essence and the pain of that moment of
birth are at the heart of creation, at the heart of a God both
male and female.*

*So in life, the metaphor of the cord, of the tie, the connec-
tion, both wholly present and wholly loosened, remains with
me as a powerful metaphor both for parenting, and for
growing, myself, as a child of God.*

Hearts haiku

Hearts beat together –
miracle umbilical
springs life between us.

*Our oldest child set off, at the age of 9, on her first school
residential. The parting, the missing and the returning spoke
to me of the ebb and flow of God's relationship with each*

one of us, a child of God, and of the ultimate glory of meeting God face-to-face.

Child of mine

Child of mine
you set off, bag in hand,
for your first post-womb solo journey.

(For you have been here before,
venturing into the unknown,
pushed, shoved, loved
beyond the womb
to an as-yet-unseen new life
where arms beckon and
hearts ache
to love you.)

Today, I release you,
I let you go.
You are mine, and yet
you are wholly your own.

Child of mine,
I miss you.
Yet in the missing
I love you
more roundly,
more deeply,
more strongly
than I could imagine.

Child of mine,
your return is as sweet
as the first sign of spring,
as the brush of a lip;
your journey across the playground,
bags now spilling from your shoulders,

spills love from my heart,
as I laugh and run to gather you up.

And in that moment,
child of mine,
I catch a glimpse of heaven,
where God will catch up
each child of Hers
and she will laugh with love
on our return.

*Becoming a mother drew me full circle to the fact of my
being mothered by God. 'Child of God' reflects this journey:*

Child of God

There is a thread that runs through my centre,
my miracle middle,
uniting creator to created.

This thread is golden, luscious, life-rich.

This thread is
the litmus,
the temperature,
the gauge
of all things spiritual and grounding.

My golden thread pulses
with life:
when my inner core resonates with an outer calling,
then I know the path, the thread, the pulse
is a life-rich path.

This I call discernment.
This is life.
This is choosing
life over death.

My golden thread never disappears,
but my goodness,
it struggles, and sputters, and is
so thin and weak that sometimes I feel
disconnected. Life-poor.

Disconnected from my thread,
I spiral, lose gravity, disconnect from
the people, the world around me.
Disconnect from my self. From my core.

As a child, born of flesh, born of God,
I give thanks for the thread that connects
creator to created.

*In a world where still the default image for God is masculine, I
relish the opportunity to reflect on the wholeness of the creator
God: mother-father-parent.*

Wholly God

With God as woman
I am much braver
when it comes
to the heart of the matter;
or rather, when it comes
to matters of the heart.

With God as woman
I throw my inhibitions
to the wind.
I sparkle
with laughter and the guts of love
as my communication.

With God as woman
life is round and full
and tears conquer fear

which trembles,
then disappears
in the presence of
such splendid
wholeness.

With God as woman
justice flows in
her desire to seek right
and good, and life for all
creation.
Energy, and anger
ride in equal place,
naming wrong, birthing life.

With God as woman
life is complete.
Nothing more.
No show.
For God is complete
in you, in me.
That's all.

Notes and sources:

Original versions of some of these poems first appeared in the books *Wrestling and Resting* (CTBI), *Acorns and Archangels*, *Pushing the Boat Out* and *Ready or Not* (Wild Goose Publications). Used by permission of Ruth Harvey.

Prayers for Holy Week

John Harvey

Palm Sunday

On this day, Jesus and his disciples entered Jerusalem to finally confront the religious authorities of the day. Jesus rode in on a donkey rather than a horse, to show that he came in peace, and the crowds welcomed him with palm branches and shouts of 'Hosanna!' Then he retired with his disciples to Bethany.

Scripture reading: Mark 11:1–11

Prayer

Jesus, Lord of the Journey,
we thank you
that you set your face firmly towards Jerusalem,
with a single eye and a pure intent,
knowing what lay ahead
but never turning aside.

Jesus, Lord of the Palms,
we thank you
that you enjoyed the shouts of 'Hosanna!'
from the ordinary people,
living fully in that moment of welcome
and accepting their praise.

Jesus, Lord of the Cross and the Empty Tomb,
we thank you
that you freely entered the heart
of our evil and our pain,
along a way that was
both terrible and wonderful,
as your kingship became your brokenness,
and your dying became
the triumph of undying love.

Monday in Holy Week

On this day, Jesus and his disciples stayed in the home of Martha, Mary and Lazarus in Bethany – where Mary anointed Jesus' feet with perfume, and wiped them with her hair.

Scripture reading: John 12:1– 7

Prayer

God of love,
in Jesus we see the true nature of your love –
vulnerable, personal, costly, setting love's standards for all time.
Look in mercy on us,
whose loving rarely even approaches the standard set by Jesus.
Forgive us –
and help us to be encouraged by the openness
Jesus showed to Martha and to Mary –
as to all who loved him, even a little, in their own way.
Help us to love a little more like Jesus,
so that the scent of love may be detected in our lives.
We ask this in Jesus' name.
Amen

Tuesday in Holy Week

On this day, Jesus and his disciples returned to Jerusalem, where he entered the Temple and overthrew the tables of the money-changers, declaring the Temple to be again a place of prayer for all nations.

Scripture reading: Mark 11:15–19

Prayer

Loving God,
you know the need we have as human beings
for things to taste and touch,
to smell and feel.
You know we are never satisfied only with words –
you made us,
body as well as spirit,
flesh as well as soul.
Thank you then for the things of our religion
that speak to us of our faith.
Cleanse our religious traditions of anything
that would turn our faith into stone;
may they always speak to us of Kingdom values –
the justice, the peace, the care for the poor,
the costly faith, that is never content
unless it is walking in the footsteps of Jesus.
We pray in his name.
Amen

Wednesday in Holy Week

On this day, Judas Iscariot entered into an agreement with the Jewish leaders to betray Jesus to them.

Scripture reading: John 13:21–30

Prayer

How much are you worth to me, Jesus?
The Gospel tells us that to Judas,
you were worth thirty pieces of silver.
Not much – a day's wages –
hardly a reason for such a betrayal.
And to the others –
the dozy eleven who fell asleep in the garden,
put on a brief show of bravado,
then forsook you and fled?
They didn't value you all that highly either, it would seem.
And what about me?
What about me, concerned, like they were,
far more with my own agenda
than with yours, most of the time?
Do I really value you above my issues, my needs,
even my understanding of the faith?

On this day, Jesus, help me admit,
yet again,
my need of your forgiving kiss,
and remind me that you value me far higher
than I deserve
or can ever repay.
Amen

Maundy Thursday

On this night, Jesus ate the Passover meal with his disciples, and washed their feet, thus inaugurating the new covenant between God and all people, which he was to seal the next day with his blood. Then he was betrayed by Judas, deserted by his disciples and handed over to be crucified.

Scripture readings: John 13:1–15, Luke 22:14–20

Prayer

Loving God,
on this night you waited, in Jesus,
for so much.

You waited for loyalty –
and found betrayal.
You waited for support –
and got, instead, desertion.
You waited for love –
and received instead
hatred, misunderstanding, rejection,
and a cruel death.

Loving God,
still you wait for us.
We are no different from your first disciples.
We carry within us all the sin that can crucify you
again and again.

Here on this night,
the night of the basin and towel,
of the bread broken and the wine outpoured,
help us to wait now on you.
Let your mercy and grace unite us in your forgiveness.
And make us one with all your suffering children
who wait for your reign of justice and peace to come
and change their lives.
We pray in Jesus' name.
Amen

Good Friday

On this day, Jesus endured the mockery of a trial; he was condemned to death, tortured and executed; then his body was taken down from the Cross, and buried in a borrowed grave.

Scripture reading: Mark 15:16–39

Prayer

Lord Jesus,
lifted high on the cross,
you look down on us in all our greatness,
and all our sin.
And in your amazing love
you sift out the good in us,
in both our greatness,
and our sin.

Look in mercy on all who need you now;
especially those who would not dream of approaching you,
who feel themselves excluded from your love.
Live for them, we pray,
as you died for them;
and have mercy on us
who go in danger of thinking ourselves good,
when you have taught us
who alone is good,
and shown us,
by your living and your dying,
how we may honour Him.
We pray in your name.
Amen

Holy Saturday

On this day, as Jesus lay, dead, in the tomb, the disciples remained scattered in fear, and the women watched, and waited …

Scripture reading: Matthew 27:57–61

Prayer

Living God, we are come,
with Joseph and the Marys,
to the place of death and despair.
With them, we have seen the awful power of hatred,
fear and greed,
having its way with frail flesh
and that once so fragrant hope.
With them, we have felt the shock of iron on bone,
of state power on puny mortals,
of religious righteousness on the faint freedom of faith.
With them we have heard that well-loved voice go silent,
seen that deeply desired face fall vacant,
the eyes grow dim,
the flesh turn cold.
Death has had its way with all that they, and we,
held most dear;
and we have felt the first fear,
the beginnings of the awful loneliness,
the emptiness
where fullness once was,
ought still to be.

Dear God, you know that we have been here before.
Been here, not just with Joseph and the Marys,

but on our own,
watching a loved one die;
or with friends and family,
paying our last respects at the door of death
to one who has gone through ahead of us all.
We are not strangers to death,
we know its ways.

Dear God, help us, now as before,
to hold our hand from any final action;
to hold our breath from any final word.
Teach us, once again,
the truth of our creatureliness:
that we are not the masters of our fate,
we are not the captains of our souls.
Keep us open to the possibilities of God
throughout this watchful night;
and in the face of every dying
with which our lives are filled from our first cry
to our final breath,
help us to know that the final word lies with you,
and that that word is a resounding YES.

We ask this in the name of this same dead Jesus
in whom all the possibilities of God wait their time.
Amen

Easter Sunday

On a day like this, the Risen Christ met with his disciples by the lake shore; together they shared a breakfast of fish and bread. Then he asked Peter if he loved him …

Scripture readings: John 20:1–2, John 21:1–14

Prayer

We thought we had heard it all, dear God,
we thought we knew!
The Bible stories; the words of our faith;
the rules for living and the way to heaven;
we thought, dear God, we knew!
But here, before the mystery again of a grave that is empty
when it should be filled with a decaying corpse,
we know we know nothing at all!
Lord, have mercy on us!

We thought we had heard it all, dear God,
we thought we knew!
The great stories of the church; the ebb and flow of the faith;
our place in the great scheme of things;
we thought, dear God, we knew!
But here, before the mystery again of death defeated,
of broken folk made whole,
and mighty powers quite broken down,
we know we know nothing at all!
Lord, have mercy on us!

We thought we had heard it all, dear God,
we thought we knew!
The way of the world; the powers that be,
and the powers that would be;
the ebb and flow of armies and international finance;
the endless tide of refugees,
and the awful endlessness of hate;

we thought, dear God, we knew!
But here, before the mystery again of a word of love in a quiet garden,
and the promise, suddenly,
of a new order of creation
in place of the old, tired, familiar scene,
we know we know nothing at all!
Lord, have mercy on us!
Have mercy on your people, Lord.

Take out our stony hearts –
our cynical, confident, controlling,
careful, cautious hearts –
and give us again hearts of flesh, we pray;
so that, knowing our own ignorance,
we may be filled instead with your knowledge;
filled with that saving knowledge
which in the beginning made all things;
that saving knowledge which in Jesus Christ,
crucified, dead and risen,
can make all things, even us, new again;
that saving knowledge which will,
in that same Christ,
bring all things, in the end,
to their completion.
In his name we pray.
Amen

Blessing

Go now before us, Risen Christ,
into the world of your loving,
the world of your living and dying,
and there, help us to bear witness to your Risen Life.
Christ be with us,
Christ within us,
Christ behind us,
Christ before us,

Christ to win us,
Christ to comfort and restore us.
Christ beneath us,
Christ above us,
Christ in quiet,
Christ in danger,
Christ in hearts of all who love us,
Christ in mouth of friend and stranger.

And the blessing of God,
Creator, Son and Spirit,
be with you,
and among you,
and go with you wherever you go,
now and always.
Amen

These are the friends

A song for Maundy Thursday
or Good Friday

Jan Sutch Pickard

(Tune: 'Waly Waly')

These are the friends that you asked to stay
and to keep watch with faithfulness:
they fell asleep, leaving you to pray,
and failed you in your deep distress.

This is the one who believed in power,
thinking your dream was the same as his,
but suffering love he could not endure:
Judas betrayed you with a kiss.

These are the followers deep in shock –
afraid to face the coming day –
the shepherd's lost to the scattered flock
for your disciples all ran away.

This is the man you called the Rock –
to found the church and defend the right –
but he denied you, until the cock
crowed Peter's failure through the night.

This is the judge who could not decide
what was the truth, what he should do;
your silence spoke to the fear inside
and Pilate washed his hands of you.

This is the crowd who were given the choice
who could go free and who should die;
for the insurgent they raised their voice,
to you they shouted 'Crucify!'

This is our story, this is our song:
we are the ones who put out the light.
Forgive us, Lord, for a world of wrong:
we all have failed, and it is night.

At the foot of the Cross

A meditation for Good Friday for several voices

Joy Mead

(Divide up the Bible readings, poems, prayers and reflections between different leaders.)

He came out and went, as was his custom, to the Mount of Olives; and the disciples followed him. When he reached the place, he said to them, 'Pray that you may not come into the time of trial.' Then he withdrew from them about a stone's throw, knelt down, and prayed, 'Father, if you are willing, remove this cup from me; yet, not my will but yours be done.' Then an angel from heaven appeared to him and gave him strength. In his anguish he prayed more earnestly, and his sweat became like great drops of blood falling down on the ground. When he got up from prayer, he came to the disciples and found them sleeping because of grief …

Luke 22:39–45 (NRSV)

Chant or short song: e.g. 'Kyrie' or 'Kyrie (Ukraine)', *Iona Abbey Music Book*, Wild Goose Publications

Legend says that while the Apostles slept in the Garden of Gethsemane, Mary and Martha were awake, watching and praying at the garden gate.

Gethsemane

At Gethsemane the skirts of light
grow wider in the immense dark,
revealing watchers at the gate.

The women there – watching, seeing,
awake: waiting without interfering
quiet in their humble love.

While sleeping men no longer attend,
the women focus wholly
on the depths of human experience.

Helpless, baffled, marginalised,
with a precious generosity
they minister with eyes and ears.

They are waiting with patient attention
for the insight not yet given;
waiting and never relinquishing

the ability to feel; never losing
the capacity for compassion
or the strength to hope;

waiting and holding on to their vision;
forever at the gate;
forever ready.

But the story won't let us stay in the garden. We must follow …

Then the soldiers of the governor took Jesus into the governor's headquarters, and they gathered the whole cohort around him. They stripped him and put a scarlet robe on him, and after twisting some thorns into a crown, they put it on his head. They put a reed in his right hand and knelt before him and mocked him, saying, 'Hail, King of the Jews!' They spat on him, and took the reed and struck him on the head. After mocking him, they stripped him of the robe and put his own clothes on him. Then they led him away to crucify him.

Matthew 27:27–31(NRSV)

Chant or short song: e.g. 'Kyrie' or 'Kyrie (Ukraine)'

Then they brought Jesus to the place called Golgotha (which means the place of a skull).

Mark 15:22 (NRSV)

Here where three crosses
are stark against the sky,
where people come and go
in malice, cruelty
and abject desolation,

is no place or time
for objectivity,
no place for reason
or logic.

Here is humanity
stripped bare, vulnerable.
See: the human story.
It's written on a body
that has been kissed
and anointed with love
and sweet perfume,
has eaten bread and wine
and washed feet.
Look:
blood and excreta,
sweat and spit,
flesh and tissue fragility;
a life, a human body, brutalised,
contorted and distorted,
spit upon, rejected.
Don't avert your gaze,
close your heart
or hide in familiar washed
and perfumed language
with comforting doctrines.
Here our elaborate theologies
clank like empty buckets.

There is no high purpose
or meaning to human cruelty,
the killing of innocent people,
all this brokenness,
all this devastation
of what is most precious.

Life isn't about meaning
it's about connections,

reaching out
not reaching up.
There is no religious
or moral rule to equal
the demands of love.

Look, see,
hold on to the messiness
and brokenness, the wholeness
of body and spirit.

> God of all love and every truth,
> help us to look with open eyes,
> see with open hearts.

Paying attention,
attending to all people
and all things in their mystery,
depth and ordinariness,
is the essence of prayer,
the rarest and purest
form of generosity.

If you turn away,
if you look for angels,
or some worldly sign,
if you separate body
and mind, then,
and only then,
can you rationalise
this or any other atrocity
the newspapers report today,
violence, abuse, oppression –
from Guantánamo Bay to Iraq
from Darfur to Zimbabwe
from Israel/Palestine
to our own backyards.
Nor is this a place for romantics:

a sanitised crucifixion
with clean, unbloodied body.
It's a place of evil,
a place of too much destruction.
Humankind cannot stand too much reality
and yet the demanding common task
is to look and to love
and cry: Mercy …

Our serious looking
has a healing beauty.
In loving-attention
is enabling grace
that tunes us into
the heart-rending harmony
of life and death.

> God of all love and every truth,
> help us to look with open eyes,
> see with open hearts.

When it was noon, darkness came over the whole land until three in the afternoon. At three o'clock Jesus cried out with a loud voice, 'Eloi, Eloi, lema sabachthani?' which means, 'My God, my God, why have you forsaken me?'

Mark 15:33,34 (NRSV)

> That huge 'Why?'
> held deep inside us all
> or spat out occasionally
> isn't an intellectual question.

> It's a cry of agony.

> There are no answers,
> only the waiting,
> the walking alongside,
> the being here.

Only the giving
out of what we do not have:
the love that comes
as we give it.
The incredible risk
of love
demands more of us
than easy answers and pretty prayers.

But all his acquaintances, including the women who had followed him
from Galilee, stood at a distance, watching these things.

Luke 23:49

Mary at the foot of the cross
waits to hold her dead son
in her arms.

Who would dare to look
into her secret eyes;
who now would dare
to sing Magnificat?
Her still body is the shape
of a multitude of grieving women.

Death does not dry her tears.
They wash over history …
into the places
words will never reach.

Woman without comfort or consolation,
she keeps a timeless vigil
for nameless mothers
and their missing sons and daughters;
for all who pick up the pieces,
collect the wounded,
bring home the dead
and wait for bread
to feed the living.

Silence

There will always be the waiting:

waiting with the dying;
waiting at the bedside of a sick child;
waiting at a peace vigil;
waiting for news of missing sons and daughters,
husbands and wives, mothers or fathers;
waiting amid illness, abuse, oppression;
waiting at the gates;
waiting at the place of desolation,
the human rubbish dump ...

There will always be the watching,
the standing alongside,
through the long night,
preparing food for the weary,
caring for the children,
encouraging with a word,
a smile ... a hug.
Presence and compassion:
not ministering to
but being with.

Joanna, Susanna and Mary

Some women of the company
watch with the angels
from their own place –
somewhere at the margins,

where bread and wine,
spices and perfumes
loving and caring
flow freely;

where they mourn;
and cry for children
living now and
yet to be born;

where seeing
into the heart
of all things
is by the clear light
beyond death

so that the margins
are becoming a new centre.
Hopes and dreams
(men call foolish nonsense)
are leading not to chapel or church,
temple or synagogue
but to the foot of a cross:
to wonder at a story
ordinary enough to live by;
to wait silently
for men to outgrow
their madness
and the sun
to rise again.

Silence

Waiting
is a sign,
a living poem.

Waiting
carries the needs
of the people
quietly within.

'They also serve who only stand and wait'
(John Milton, Sonnet XVI)

Weep over injustice,
rejoice in goodness,
love outrageously.
Let uncertainty flow
on the stillness
of our bodies

for we know not what we do …
nor what we can do.

God of all love and every truth,
help us to look with open eyes,
see with open hearts.

Then Jesus, crying with a loud voice, said, 'Father, into your hands I commend my spirit.' Having said this, he breathed his last. When the centurion saw what had taken place, he praised God and said, 'Certainly this man was innocent.'

Luke 23:46,47 (NRSV)

We are stretched between
the motionless point we watch,
the cry of humanity,
and the common task
to make a better world.

Never turning away from suffering,
always able to see what is
and imagine how things
could be different,
holding hands with those who wait –
family, friend, stranger, and some
from whom we might recoil –
we seek words good enough
to tell a story to live by.

Words like love, fragility, vulnerability,
uncertainty and solidarity.
These tell of God,

of selfless acts
that free and transform,
of ordinary people
around the world
forming co-ops, campaign groups,
self-help groups, organising protests
and peace marches,
seeking an end to poverty, oppression
social marginalisation
and environmental devastation.

We wait – and look again
not so much at what we believe,
but how we see, hear and understand
what it means to be alive and open

to that which is deepest within us,
that which responds to life,
that which responds with all our being
to other people and the world
around us in its joy …
and in its agony.
There is at large in the world
amazing imaginative power
to reinvent ourselves,
to re-make the world.

We know we are in the dark
but perhaps that is a good place to be,
a good place from which to tell
of ongoing and energising hope
and love strong enough
to banish fear and bear regrets.
What do we expect to achieve?

We don't know.
Waiting at the foot of the cross
is being on the edge of something
not quite revealed.

We're still in the dark.

But hope isn't about expectations –
as the Jesus stories show us –
it's about surprises!

Surprise

Dandelions on dung heaps;
daisies in stone walls;
the long goodwill
of the damp-floored forest
where old leaves
nurture new trees
and the hopeful energy
of creativity's seedbed
nourishes the silent outrage
of spring;

these chip away at petrified logic
and play with reason's straightjacket;
outgrow the private;

make me face my own name
as if it belongs
somewhere else;

make me lose myself
in the huge surprise of life
in the jack-in-the-box,
head-over-heels world
of multi-coloured movement
that outbursts
the first
and every
'I love you'.

Transformation begins with people of love, discernment, joy, hope ...
with compassion as the only way to grow.
The earth is waiting.
In the caring and the waiting
we are one with all growing, living things –
people in the dark who feel the coming of the dawn ...

Iona dawn

I am waiting by the shore
in the early darkness
when the rising sun
touches a broken world,
makes a flame
of each blade of grass,
warms the silent stones,
sends larks up
into the clean air.

The new day miracle
and the end of waiting:
I am emptied wholly
into a moment of wonder
with no desire to make sense
of all this light.

Chant or short song: e.g. 'Kyrie' or 'Kyrie (Ukraine)'

Good Friday and Holy Saturday

Three reflections

Jan Sutch Pickard

I thirst

'I thirst' (John 19:28, KJB/AV)

I thirst

The heat of the midday sun beats back
from the bare rocks of this hilltop,
from the bleached wood of this cross.
The last time this man saw water
was when Pilate washed the blood-guilt from his hands.
The last time it passed these cracked lips
was at table with his friends –
who have now run away like raindrops into the thirsty earth.

I thirst

He imagines water flowing down a riverbed
after the spring rains, when the land is green,
where trees grow at the water's edge,
and – watched by kingfishers in their branches
and by crowds from the city along the bank –
two men wade into the Jordan,
waist-deep in the still unpolluted waters.
John cupped his hand and raised it,
a rosary of bright drops falling as he poured water
over this head that is now beaded with blood.
Then the dove came down out of a clear heaven
and a voice proclaimed, 'This is my beloved son ...'
But now the only words under the empty sky are

I thirst

'Son,' said his mother at the wedding,
'there is no wine left!'
And he laughed, 'What's that to me?'
But now, when his hour has come, he remembers
that in the courtyard there stood six stone water jars –
huge and full to the brim with cool pure water –

and that he sent the servants
to draw all the wine that they wanted –
to quench everyone's thirst,
enliven the party and celebrate human love.
That was a sign, water into wine,
just as much as the voice from heaven.
Folk said then that the host had left the best till last.
But at last, for the man on the cross, water will do:

I thirst

'Give me a drink,' he had said
to the woman at the well outside the city;
her look mingled wonder and mockery:
'You, a Jewish man, ask for a drink from a Samaritan woman?'
So many prejudices, prohibitions, dangers of misunderstanding.
Water was the one simple thing.
He remembers how thirsty he was,
sitting there by the well.
She drew water out of its depths,
the bucket overflowing, splashing, echoing,
precious water coming up dark and then flashing gold
as she poured it out in the sunshine.
The traveller drank his fill,
letting it caress his throat, grinning in gratitude,
splashing it on his face, his hands, his dusty feet,
making free with the water that was her gift.
Then the talk turned to living water –
a gift to her she didn't, at first, understand.
But she had understood his human need:

I thirst

His friends hadn't understood,
when he took the basin and the towel,
and washed their feet.
The upper room was filled with baffled silence,
the slip-slop of water, words of protest,

uncertain laughter. But his gentle hands
turned a routine task into a sign of caring:
the water blessed them, brought them together.
Though they drank wine that night,
for some the water was what they remembered:
the washing, the water poured out for them.
And it went on flowing through their lives.
As his life ebbs, he calls out again

I thirst

The soldiers raise a sponge soaked in sour wine, vinegar,
to his parched lips. It is as sharp
as the barbed wire and the minefields along the Jordan;
as cheap as booze which people drink to forget
and as stale as a marriage that doesn't work out;
as bitter as the divisions between men and women,
rich and poor, races, different faiths;
it silences the cry for justice
and it leaves a bad taste in the mouth;
it is as numbing as our guilt, as our fear of being loved.

This man's life was living water. Is this the last word?

I thirst

Drawing on John 19:28–30; John 1:31–33; John 2:1–11; John 4:4–15; John 13:3–15

Words from the Cross

(John 19:30b)

Jesus said, 'It is finished.'
Then he bowed his head and gave up his spirit.

This is the end
and we will all come to it.
We are mortal. Our bodies wear out,
cannot stand the strain and shock
of the world in which we live as mortal beings.
In Jesus, God entered our mortality,
crept into this fragile shell
which is unique, beautiful, but not eternal.
We exist in time.
Jesus lived in a particular time and place,
and died at a moment of time,
as each of us will do.

But how he died!
He died alone
and yet with all eyes on him
in anguish, in terror,
in love, in despair.
We cannot know what was in his mind
any more than the figures falling –
arms outstretched through space –
from the burning tower
on a day we can never forget.
A day fixed in time.

But we remember now
that there was another moment in time
after which nothing would ever be the same:
when the man Jesus cried, 'It is finished'
and fell out of the world.
Out of time.

Leaving a great emptiness
and silence.

Jesus said, 'It is finished.'
Then he bowed his head and gave up his spirit.

Holy Saturday

(Mark 15:40–16:2)

Here we are
in the waiting room: the place
where everyone is a stranger; the space
between death and burial.

Numbness and
no-man's-land.

We women kept watch
while Joseph from Arimathaea
went to ask for the body.
He has become an undertaker –
the borrowed tomb
a chapel of rest –
because now we are entering
a day of rest,
when even this task,
this last loving ministry,
must be left half-done.

Mourning is put on hold.

Death is a hard fact –
but somehow we need to touch it
one more time, to know
its finality, to show
our respect, to let go.

Meanwhile the story is incomplete.

We, the women, go on watching,
waiting for the Sabbath to be over,
so that we can return

with spices, at dawn
on the first day of the week –
and know for sure

it is finished:
the one we love is not there …
know there's nothing to wait for any more.

Sources:

Originally from the books *We Journey in Hope*, Peter Millar and Neil Paynter (Eds), Wild Goose Publications, and *Out of Iona*, Jan Sutch Pickard, WIld Goose Publications.

It wasn't the nails

A reflection and prayers
on the Cross

David Rhodes

Reflection:

It wasn't the nails, though they were bad enough. It was his head. And it seemed to be getting worse.

When he tried to rest his head against the wood there had been a blinding pain that made him cry out.

It had started with the beating. Blindfolded and tied to a chair in a cell. Then the blows to the head, never knowing where the next one was coming from.

Finally, the hammer blow and the crack of fractured bone. What was that? The centurion's heavy, swagger stick? The man must have lost his temper, furious that they could not break his will.

Now it is almost over. The ground seems a long way below him. The women are there, determined and defiant as ever. And a handful of ragged children. Street urchins who have pushed and wriggled through to the front of the crowd. Of such is the …

One of the other men being executed shouts angrily, resentfully, accusingly:

'Save yourself – and save us.' And his unspoken words: *Why did you not join us? You could have led us in the fight for freedom – for justice.*

There is silence. The words are more painful than the wounds. Maybe he's right. Perhaps it would have been different. But armed struggle is never the answer.

The darkness is closing in now. My God, my God, it is cold. Why have they forsaken me? If feels almost as if God has forsaken me.

The ordeal seems endless, but he knows they do not want him dead. It sounds bizarre but he is probably the only man they ever crucified and did not want dead. They want more than death. They want him to beg for his life. To sell his soul. Say it was all a sham. Confess. Change sides. Turn traitor. Bow down and worship Caesar.

Back on the mountaintop: *'All this I will, we give you, if you will ...'*

Deep in his thoughts, he almost misses it:

Someone calling his name. The other political prisoner, freedom-fighter, zealot. Whatever. But not a criminal. He is shouting hoarsely. Urgently:

'Jesus, remember me.' Remember me. Remember me.

Remember you when, my brother?

'When you come into your Kingdom.'

When? Did you say *when* ... not *if*? Are you so sure?

A shaft of light pierces the darkness. It's not so cold now.

He looks down at the ground far below. There is no sign of the Twelve. Only the women. One of the children has edged closer. The guards seem not to have noticed her, she is so small and thin.

She stands staring up, but not at him. She is staring at the other man. Registering what he has said. Remember. Remember me. Remember me *when* ...

He can see it in her eyes. She is not watching: she is listening. Listening intently. Lost in the moment. Remember. Remember this.

A woman comes up and takes her hand. She too is listening, as the women always do. While the famous Twelve had argued and boasted, the women listened.

Maybe all is not lost. Maybe the women. And a child ...

Shall the last be first, after all? He smiles.

And then he died.

Confession:

Lord, what can we say?
Two thousand years of worship;
two thousand years of invoking the name of Jesus,
and the world is a disaster zone.
Greed, pollution, famine and endless wars.
Suddenly the words 'The End is nigh'
don't sound so crazy after all.

You asked for love and we gave respectability;
you asked for justice and we gave selfishness and insularity;
you asked for compassion and we spread fear;
you asked us to care for our neighbours
but we stole their food and their dignity.
You raised Jesus from the dead
but we buried him again in religion.

Lord, what can we say?
Perhaps 'sorry' would be a start.
But how can we confess our failings
when we find it so hard to feel regret?
Maybe we should simply kneel before you in silence
and let you do the talking.

Lord, have mercy ...

Prayers on crucifixion:

It's easy to think of the Crucifixion as something that happened a long time ago. But for some people every day is Good Friday. People forced into poverty, those who are homeless. Those seeking asylum. People crushed by debt and treated with contempt by the powerful. Jesus is crucified today in their suffering …

Asylum seekers:

Lord, it's so easy to think of asylum seekers
(when we think of them at all)
as Other.
As foreign.
Different in colour and perhaps religion.
We think of them as distant.
We are tempted to think of them coming to 'our' country.
Yes, there's distance and a feeling of separation in the idea of asylum.
But help us, Lord, to remember that,
at the hour of our own death,
we ourselves will be asylum seekers.
Hoping and praying for sanctuary
and a loving welcome with you in heaven.
Let our own mortality help us to be one
with those who seek asylum in Britain today.
And let us offer them gladly
the hospitality of love
that is your gift to us all.
Amen

Debt:

Why did we do it, Lord?
Rewrite your prayer.
You said cancel our debts,
but we preferred forgive us our trespasses.
Which sounds a lot more dignified.
Moderate. Respectable.

But you, it seems, said debts –
and you said it to people experiencing crushing debt.
Debt that brought dishonour, destitution and death.
We prefer the calm of organised religion,
but your focus was on organised greed and oppression.
Debt is still with us today – in spades.
Help us, Lord, to remember that debt and the struggle for justice
are at the heart of our spirituality.
And at the heart of Your Prayer.
Amen

Food banks:

OK, Lord, we've got it now.
Money banks are bad, food banks are good.
And, it has to be said,
food banks certainly help people: lots of hungry people.
They're a symbol of caring and compassion.
So, why didn't you set up food banks, Lord?
Or walk-in clinics, come to that?
There were vast numbers of hungry and sick people
in first-century Palestine.
It's only very gradually we realise
your miracles were a sign not a solution.
Your solution was an end to injustice and oppression.
But that threatened the system:
the system operated by the rich and powerful.
Looking back on all that,
it's clear that the Cross was inevitable.
But no one is likely to get crucified for running a food bank.
Which should make us think.
Maybe we need to go beyond the Good Samaritan, as you did.
Amen

The homeless:

Lord, there's a children's game of skimming flat pebbles across a lake:
watching them bounce along its surface.
Maybe you played the game as a child at the Sea of Galilee.
The trouble is, Lord,
we play that game with the Gospel.
We skim over it.
You said 'the son of man has nowhere to lay his head'.
We read those familiar words,
but we don't want to let them sink in.
We don't really take in the fact
that you were often homeless:
no shelter, no bed, no toilet paper.
You were alongside the homeless.
And they, in turn, gave you loyalty and love.
Today you meet us among the homeless.
And in that encounter,
we discover the depth of your love –
for them and for ourselves.
Amen

The living wage:

They were a great idea, Lord.
Your parables.
Simple stories with simple messages.
But it seems we still manage to get them wrong.
The labourers in the vineyard, for example.
Was that about a generous landowner?
An image of God himself?
Or was it about exploitation:
a rich man paying starvation wages to zero-hours labourers?
And then, on top of that,
setting them at each other's throats?
Was there a hard edge to your story?

One that the poor
and those turned off their land
would have recognised?

You came that we may have life.
All of us.
That means justice, respect
and a 'living' wage.
A life-giving wage.
In a world of plenty,
anything less than that is an injustice.
A denial of your promise.
God's promise.
Amen

Welfare and work:

Lord, why do so many people snigger
at the mention of health and safety?
Isn't that exactly what we wish for our loved ones?
We care about their well-being.
Their welfare.
That's what love means, isn't it?
So how is it that 'welfare' has become such a dirty word
in the tabloids and in the mouths of so many politicians?
An insult. A judgement.
An expression of sneering contempt.
But you were born into the world
because of the Father's concern for our welfare.
Our well-being.
Our shalom.

Lord, let us find useful, meaningful work as we can,
but let us always seek the welfare, the health and the safety,
of our neighbour.
Even of our politicians.
Amen

Child poverty:

Lord, it's amazing that many centuries ago we started
cutting and pasting the Gospel.
The bits we were uncomfortable with got deleted:
at least in our minds.
Like when you said
you came to bring good news to the poor.
But we deleted 'to the poor'
and inserted the words: to us.
You said the last shall be first.
But a church controlled by men
never asked who 'the last' actually were.
They were the women and the children:
the ones without power.
Maybe those at the foot of the cross.
So when we pray for an end to child poverty,
help us to remember, Lord,
that in those words we come very close to your love,
your pain –
and to your anger at injustice.
Amen

Pentecost as a template

A Bible study

Ian M Fraser

Hierarchy in the church is a late and dodgy development. The Council of Trent's affirmation that Jesus Christ established a hierarchical church runs counter to all evidence. What the church has become in history has to be compared with how it was founded, to get a reckoning of whether what has been shaping it in history remains true to its origins.

In anticipation of Pentecost, the risen Christ warns disciples to leave to God what is *'set by the Father's own authority'*. They had to concentrate on what was *'for them'*, witnessing to Christ to the ends of the earth.

Thus Pentecost, as arranged and timed in a way which appertained to God's authority alone, must be thought of as a template against which the significance of variations throughout history can be assessed.

The event itself was experienced by around 120 people, of which the original band of apostles was just an element, not specially differentiated from all others. Fronds of fire touched to new life women and men, young and old, furnishing them with a variety of gifts which provided for a great variety of ministries which added up to one definitive ministry: that of the whole People of God, in double harness with the High Priesthood of Jesus Christ. They are *'a chosen race, a royal priesthood, a holy nation, God's own people'* (1 Peter 2:9, NRSV).

It is in harmony with this understanding that Paul likens the church to a body with limbs and organs which serve one another and receive from one another, related to one Head, Jesus Christ – every part contributing to the life of the whole. Worship and service express love for the world God so loved as to send the Son. Members of the body which seem to be weaker are *'indispensable … so that there should be no division in the body but that its parts should have equal concern for each other'* (see 1 Corinthians 12).

There is no superiority or inferiority, no grading of importance in functions. So there is no need for leadership?

Paul differs, and indicates immediately the forms of leadership and their character. What there is no need for is superstructure. *'God has appointed first apostles, second prophets, third teachers, then deeds of power, then gifts of healing, forms of assistance, forms of leadership, various kinds of tongues.'* He again picks up the leadership question in Ephesians 4:11, this time indicating the nature of the exercise of leadership for which some are gifted. *'The gifts that he gave were that some would be apostles, some prophets, some evangelists, some pastors and teachers, to equip the saints (i.e. the punters) for the work of ministry, for building up the body of Christ.'* The idea that those of us who are ordained are endowed with a special character beyond that of others is refuted in the original wording. Where the AV says that Jesus ordained apostles to be with him, the word 'ordained' in modern translations is given simply as 'appointed': because that is all that is meant in the text. Ordination is simply *'the action of admitting a candidate to the ministry of the church'* (*A Dictionary of Christian Theology*). That ministry is not superior over others in its character but an enabling one *'to equip ordinary believers for the work of ministry'*. The definitive ministry is that of the whole People of God.

Worship is to be built up accordingly. In 1 Corinthians 14:26 the description of worship is prefixed by the word *hotan* ('every time')*: 'every time you come together, each one has a hymn, a lesson, a revelation, a tongue or an interpretation. Let all things be done for building up the church'* – indicating that the normal form of worship is fully participatory. Folk do not have some superior agent to 'do it for them'. They enrich the worship by contributing according to their different gifts of the Spirit. Go to worship in Iona Abbey. The service might be led by a minister, or a cook, or a gardener, or a housekeeper or a maintenance man ...

So the church which developed directly from Pentecost had no command structure necessarily involving superiority and inferiority.

What happened after some time was that a male way of dealing with life asserted itself over the male/female collaborative contribution, which Genesis 1 affirms belongs to the way the world is ordered. By God's own authority the world is so constituted that male and female are to bring complementary gifts to implement God's intention for it. By God's own choice it is women and men together who are invited to be cooperators with God in bringing the Kingdom to fruition.

Jesus gave women the same dignity as men in his earthly life. In his resurrected life he left signs which gave women equal status in the new dispensation, which was not afforded them in common social currency. Paul called them *'co-workers'*. But a male backlash is shown in 1 Corinthians 15 where Paul speaks of the faith tradition as he received it, where the distinctive role of women has been airbrushed out. The practice in the new dispensation of women praying and prophesying in church (see 1 Corinthians 11:5) is attacked by whoever wrote 1 Timothy (2:11): *'Let a woman learn in silence with full submission.'* And so on … By the time we get to 80 or 100 years after Pentecost men dominate, not only shaping the church their way, but doing so – discarding the Pentecost experience and horizontal develop-ment in house churches for the pagan, imperial God/emperor/subject-people form expressed as God/Bishop/subject church.

The way the rulers of the Gentiles work their will and still want to be treated as benefactors is rejected by Jesus' followers. Top-down gradings of rank are out, and are to be ousted. You can't take the way of a servant/slave, Jesus' way, and have a pyramid of importance with higher and lower grades. (Pope John Paul II must surely have been off guard when he called cardinals 'Princes of the Church' – admitting intrusive secular influence!)

In brief, at Pentecost a community of brothers and sisters in Christ came into being *'all one in Christ Jesus'*. The whole church, not just official appointees, needs to make a new start, with women and men imaging the church with Pentecost as the corrective template.

The laity are the People of God, the whole people, the *laos*. As well ask about the role of laity in the church as about the role of water in a river. Ecclesiastics should not pretend to have separate status as church directors and spokespersons. It would be a start in the right direction if they got to know the membership so as to encourage those with appropriate compe-tence in different fields to speak from a faith basis, in place of themselves, and to bring into play the Spirit-endowed gifts of the people to build up worship as in 1 Corinthians 14 … and let the church be the church.

Prayer

Father, Son and Holy Spirit,
we confess that we celebrate Pentecost
yet fail to express in our practice the reality
that the fire of the Spirit descended on everyone present,
conferring gifts for building up the church for ministry in the world;
that while we give thanks for those who are deservedly prominent,
who sustain and enlarge our vision,
we too often neglect those gifts distributed among your people
which need to be identified, matured and brought into play.

We give thanks for basic Christian communities,
house churches and Family Groups
where different gifts are shared
and even the shy have their silence and thoughtfulness
made a creative contribution.
Save us from being like a ship laden with fruit
whose crew and passengers starve.
Hold before us the Corinthian sign:

'Every time you come together
each one has a hymn,
a lesson, a revelation,
a tongue or its interpretation.
Bring everything to bear
for building up the church.' (1 Cor 14:26)

Make us teachable before that word, we pray.
We ask it in Jesus Christ's name.
Amen

Journey towards Pentecost

A nine-day devotional

Kathryn Turner/Wellspring

Introduction

This piece can be adapted for individual or group use. The devotional begins on the day after Ascension Thursday and finishes on the day before Pentecost Sunday.

We are told that after the Ascension the disciples returned to Jerusalem and spent time together in prayer. They probably also shared stories of Jesus and of all the things they had heard him say.

Over the next nine days we will use the Gospel as a starting point for a time of reflection and prayer. The devotional is designed to be flexible: use as much or as little as you wish in your journey towards Pentecost.

The outline for each day:

Reading: a short extract from the Gospel, with reference to the full text

Wondering: a few questions relating to the reading

Contemplation: Lectio Divina (the slow, prayerful reading of the scriptures)/Gospel contemplation (putting yourself in the scene)

Reflection: some thoughts and questions

Prayer: concerns and a prayer invoking the Holy Spirit

Throughout the devotional you might find it helpful to keep a prayer journal.

The first day

Reading: John 16:21–23 (NRSV)

Jesus said to his disciples: 'When a woman is in labour, she has pain, because her hour has come. But when her child is born, she no longer remembers the anguish because of the joy of having brought a human being into the world. So you have pain now; but I will see you again, and your hearts will rejoice, and no one will take your joy from you. On that day you will ask nothing of me. Very truly, I tell you, if you ask anything of the Father in my name, he will give it to you.'

Wondering:

How does this image of a woman giving birth speak to me? Have I experienced or witnessed a birth – and do I agree with Jesus? How can I help to support people through the process of 'birth': easing their pain and encouraging them through what may be a very difficult time?

Contemplation:

Read the passage through slowly and see if any words or phrases stand out for you. Why might they have spoken to you at this time? Do they offer any insights into what God might be asking of you? …

Jesus is speaking these words as part of what is called 'the last discourse': trying to talk about things the disciples may not have understood, but would come to understand after the Resurrection and, especially, after Pentecost.

Try to put yourself in their shoes …

Imagine how the day after the Ascension would have felt to the disciples: they knew something was going to happen but not what or when. What might they have said to encourage each other, as they waited for this 'something' to happen?

Reflection:

This may not be the most comfortable Gospel reading to begin our devotion with – but speaking about birth gives us hope.

Like a woman wondering or worrying about how she will cope with a difficult labour, some people feel apprehension about the future. Others feel more excited at the prospect of new possibilities, and see great opportunity beyond any initial pain. How do you feel about the prospect and process of 'birth'?

Prayer:

Pray for those for whom the future looks worrying – even terrifying. Pray for their consolation and comfort.

Come, Holy Spirit,
to all who are preparing to give birth to new ideas
and ways of being.
Give comfort to those who are apprehensive,
confidence to those preparing for change
and trust in your guidance.

Lord's Prayer

The second day

Reading: from John 16:23–28 (NRSV)

'On that day you will ask nothing of me. Very truly, I tell you, if you ask anything of the Father in my name, he will give it to you. Until now you have not asked for anything in my name. Ask and you will receive, so that your joy may be complete.'

Wondering:

Praying in Jesus' name – what does this mean? When Peter prayed in the name of Jesus, folk were healed – the dead were raised ... How has God used my prayer? Was it as I expected – or surprising – or confusing ... but ultimately the 'right' answer?

Contemplation:

Read the passage or whole reading through slowly and see if any words or phrases stand out for you. This Gospel follows on directly from yesterday's. Do any of your thoughts today add to those from then? ...

Read the Bible passage and build up the scene in your imagination: some-times seeing the scene, as a film director might, can help to get inside it. Listen to Jesus talking to the disciples ... and then invite him to speak to you ... What does he say?

Reflection:

Prayer is powerful – but when we pray we often can't see 'the big picture'. How do you cope with this? How easy is it for you to 'let go and let God'?

Prayer:

Pray for those who have had to try to take the big picture into account, and are concerned about how their decisions will be received.

Come, Holy Spirit:
fill the hearts of your faithful.
Bless those charged with discernment about major decisions.
Grant them insight and wisdom
and a deep love of the people entrusted to them.

Lord's Prayer

The third day

Reading: from John 17:1–10 (NRSV)

After Jesus had spoken these words, he looked up to heaven and said, 'Father, the hour has come; glorify your Son so that the Son may glorify you, since you have given him authority over all people, to give eternal life to all whom you have given him. And this is eternal life, that they may know you, the only true God, and Jesus Christ whom you have sent.'

Wondering:

What does eternal life mean to me? How does the promise of eternal life influence how I live? Do I try to share that promise with others? How?

Contemplation:

Read the passage or whole reading through slowly and make a note of any words or phrases that stand out for you. Why do those words speak to you at this time? …

Take a few moments to build up the scene of Jesus praying for his disciples and try to put yourself into it. What do you see, smell, sense …? Hear Jesus say these words directly to you, perhaps looking into your eyes. What do the words mean to you now?

Reflection:

Eternal life is what we are promised at our baptism. In the constant routine or struggle of our day-to-day lives it is easy to forget our destiny. In times of change we can also lose sight of our ultimate goal and focus solely on the here and now. How can we retain a sense of vision: seeing beyond what may seem confusing or problematic? How can we help others to set things in a greater context?

Prayer

Pray for your community and its sense of vision.

Pray for an increased awareness of your eternal destiny and that of others.

Come, Holy Spirit,
and renew our vision:
remind us of the great promise made to us in baptism –
the promise of eternal life.

Lord's Prayer

The fourth day

Reading: from John 16:29–33 (NRSV)

Jesus answered them … 'I have said this to you, so that in me you may have peace. In the world you face persecution. But take courage; I have conquered the world!'

Wondering:

Jesus said many things to his disciples – and these things have been passed on to us. Which of Jesus' words have offered me comfort? Which have challenged me? Which have brought me peace? …

Contemplation:

Read the passage or whole reading a few times. Take your time and stay with any words or phrases that stand out for you. Why might those words be significant to you at this time? …

Create a setting in which Jesus might have said these words: think about the sky and surroundings, the sounds and smells … Where is Jesus: is he sitting or standing? Where are the disciples? Jesus is preparing to leave the disciples – things are going to happen that will terrify them. What expressions do you see on the faces of those around you? What is Jesus' expression? You might like to 'talk' to Jesus about anything that troubles you and invite his response.

Reflection:

Change can be frightening. People can become confused, and suspicious of the motives of others and reasons behind their decisions. At a time of major change there are doubts and uncertainties – some expressed, others hidden. This is a time for bravery: for facing the future in the knowledge that Jesus has indeed conquered the world, and given us the Spirit to help us play our part in the building up of his church. What part are you being called to play?

Prayer:

Pray for those who will have to make brave decisions over coming months.

Pray for a generosity of spirit: for trust in the work of the Holy Spirit.

Come, Holy Spirit:
deepen our faith in the One who created us,
confidence in the One who saved us
and fill our hearts with your peace.

Lord's Prayer

The fifth day

Reading: from John 17:1–11(NRSV)

Jesus looked up to heaven and said … 'Now they know that everything you have given me is from you; for the words that you gave to me I have given to them, and they have received them and know in truth that I came from you; and they have believed that you sent me.'

Wondering:

How did the disciples know that Jesus had come from the Father? What Godly qualities did they recognise in him? What helps me to believe that Jesus came from the Father and choose to follow his teaching?

Contemplation:

Read the passage or whole reading and see if any words or phrases stand out for you. Why do these words have special meaning for you today? …

Build up the scene in your imagination. Picture Jesus amongst the disciples … How does he look? What does he sound like? As you look and listen, what strikes you? What is it about Jesus that reveals the divine in him?

Reflection:

Jesus' teaching has been handed on from apostle to apostle, disciple to disciple. Over the centuries, people have gathered, prayed, discussed and discerned. How can we continue to grow in discipleship and responsibility? How can we foster a practice of discernment rooted in scripture and tradition?

Prayer:

Pray for the gift of openness to the Word of God and willingness to be guided by it.

Come, Holy Spirit:
inspire our minds with love for the Word of God,
for the rich heritage of tradition,
for the people with whom we pray and worship,
and for those with whom we long to share
the Good News at the heart of our faith.

Lord's Prayer

The sixth day

Reading: from John 17:11–19 (NRSV)

'I am not asking you to take them out of the world, but I ask you to protect them from the evil one. They do not belong to the world, just as I do not belong to the world. Sanctify them in the truth; your word is truth.'

Wondering:

What does it mean to 'not belong to the world'? How does my life show that I have been consecrated in the truth? How does the life of my community witness to the truth? How am I protected from 'the evil one'?

Contemplation:

Read the passage or whole reading through slowly and see if any words or phrases stand out for you …

Contemplate the scene. You might like to speak Jesus' words aloud: savour them … As you say the words, how do they touch you? What expression comes into your voice? How might that be an echo of the voice of Jesus?

Reflection:

We are, it is often said, *'in the world but not of it'* – a phrase that comes down the centuries to us from Jesus. What does it mean? Our contemplative communities are certainly clear signs of one way of living this truth. But how are lay people called to live in the world: 'to be in it but not of it'?

Prayer:

Come, Holy Spirit:
fill the hearts of your faithful.
Consecrate us afresh in your truth,
protect us from the temptations of our time
and show us ways in which to make our world
a better and happier place.

Lord's Prayer

The seventh day

Reading: from John 17:20–26 (NRSV)

Jesus looked up to heaven and said … 'I ask not only on behalf of these, but also on behalf of those who will believe in me through their word, that they may all be one. As you, Father, are in me and I am in you, may they also be in us, so that the world may believe that you have sent me.'

Wondering:

How do my words and actions bring others to believe in God? How have the words and actions of others helped me to believe?

Contemplation:

Read the passage or whole reading through slowly and prayerfully. Stay with any words or phrases that stand out for you and allow God to speak to you through them …

For several days now in our readings, John has described Jesus as raising his eyes to heaven. Take a moment to watch the sky: the changing patterns of cloud; the starlight and moonlight … People long believed that heaven was in the sky: we have a different sense of heaven. Allow the time of gazing up and contemplating the sky to speak to your soul of heaven and the promise of eternal joy; of wonder and of being fully present in the moment: the miraculous here and now …

Reflection:

It is a staggering thought that our lives can touch other people's lives in ways that speak to them of God: the fact that we may say or do something that helps people come to know Jesus, and that kindles the spark the Spirit has planted in them.

How can we better build up relationships of encouragement and support?

Prayer:

Pray for people in neighbouring communities or parishes.

Pray for wisdom and enthusiasm for people working together on community projects: food co-ops, youth projects, peace and justice groups ...

Come, Holy Spirit:
give us a sense of unity and common purpose;
as we have received faith through other people,
give us words and actions
that will help others to believe in you.

Lord's Prayer

The eighth day

Reading: from John 21:15–19 (NRSV)

Jesus said to Simon Peter, 'Simon son of John, do you love me more than these?' He said to him, 'Yes, Lord; you know that I love you.' Jesus said to him, 'Feed my lambs.' A second time he said to him, 'Simon son of John, do you love me?' He said to him, 'Yes, Lord; you know that I love you.' Jesus said to him, 'Tend my sheep.' He said to him the third time, 'Simon son of John, do you love me?' Peter felt hurt because he said to him the third time, 'Do you love me?' And he said to him, 'Lord, you know everything; you know that I love you.' Jesus said to him, 'Feed my sheep.'

Wondering:

We move away from 'the last discourse' to a reading that reminds us of the commission given to Peter and his successors.

How aware am I of being part of the two thousand years of the history of Christianity? How am I playing my part in witnessing to the Gospel and in building up the contemporary church?

Contemplation:

Read through the Gospel passage or whole reading and see what words or phrases speak to you. Why might these words be significant for you today? ...

Spend some time imagining the scene. Where is it set? What do you see, smell, hear ...? Where are Peter and Jesus in relation to the other disciples? What emotions do you sense: in the disciples, in Peter and in Jesus?

Reflection:

Although the call to 'feed my lambs', 'feed my sheep' was given to Peter in a very special way, it is one given to all Christians.

We express our love for Christ by feeding the hungry amongst us (Matthew 25:31–46). Who are the hungry amongst us: the homeless, the dispossessed, the lonely ...?

In order to get strength to go out and feed others, it is important to remember to feed yourself. How do you feed yourself: through contemplation, reflection, prayer, worship and communion, reading, play, conversation ...? Where do you find inspiration? ...

Prayer:

Come, Holy Spirit:
fill the hearts of your faithful.
Give us ears to hear the call of Jesus
and minds, hearts and wills
ready and willing
to respond to it.

Lord's Prayer

The ninth day

Reading: from John 21:20–25 (NRSV)

This is the disciple who is testifying to these things and has written them, and we know that his testimony is true. But there are also many other things that Jesus did; if every one of them were written down, I suppose that the world itself could not contain the books that would be written.

Wondering:

What were all the 'other things' that Jesus did and said? Why did John and the other Gospel writers choose the stories and sayings they did? Ask yourself: If I had been an eyewitness to the events in Jesus' lifetime, which story/saying would I be most keen to have included in a Gospel? Why?

Contemplation:

Read the passage or whole reading through slowly. What words or phrases stand out for you? Let the words sink into your soul, allowing God to speak to you through them …

Call to mind some of your favourite accounts of events in the Gospel or your favourite sayings of Jesus. Spend a while with one of them, building up the scene in your imagination – seeing and hearing Jesus in action or at prayer. Invite him to share anything that he wants you to know; or place before him a concern or worry and ask him for new insights or advice.

Reflection:

Tomorrow is Pentecost Sunday, and so our devotional is drawing to a close. But our journey does not end here. Our times of prayer have helped to prepare us for a new beginning – a new Pentecost. Like the early Christians, we will of course experience uncertainties; there will be disagreements and the need to take time to build up trust and new relationships. But we do this having reflected on events in Jesus' life, which offer both challenge and great promise.

Prayer:

Give thanks for the joy of people who are witnessing God's promises being fulfilled.

Come, Holy Spirit:
fill the hearts of your faithful
and kindle in them your love.
Send forth your Spirit to re-create us
and renew the face of the earth.

Lord's Prayer

Source:

The day of the vision

A dramatic reading and prayers
on Acts 10

Chris Polhill

These resources could be used as part of a Pentecost service or Communion.

Collect:

Living God,
grant us the grace of true vision
so we may serve your people:
so the Good News is heard today,
lived in our locality,
bringing your healing and justice.
For the sake of your kin-dom on earth.
Amen

Opening prayer:

Holy God,
you challenge ordinary people
to live in your truth and love.
As we worship you today,
touch our hearts
with your bright fire,
that we may live the vision
that fits your knowing of us.
Amen

Suggested Bible readings: Proverbs 29:18 (KJV); Acts 10; Acts 2:14–21; Acts 16:6–10; Acts 18:5–11; Acts 26:2– 23

The day of the vision (on Acts 10)

I've served Cornelius for as long as I can remember. He has always treated me well, even though I'm a slave. A good master to serve: reasonable and just. Prayed too, not just for show or from fear but from love of God. Nothing wrong in that. It did no harm and maybe even some good. He certainly gave more to charity than some I could mention. Though it all meant little to me – the gods were not for the likes of me. That was my thinking anyway, till the day of the vision.

I'd been to the market for the mistress and set some lads chopping wood, and was just crossing the hall to slip down to the cellar, just to be out of the way – it being nice and cool down there … No, nothing to do with the wine barrel – and you have no call to suggest it. I was just crossing the hall – when the master comes stumbling down the stairs as white as a sheet. At first I thought he was drunk, then I thought he was ill, and as I hurried over to help him he says, all hoarse and out of breath, that I'm to go and fetch 'Peter from Joppa'. I stared at him thinking he must be out of his mind – who, what? – when he seems to pull himself together a bit, and sends me off to fetch Marcus and Kedar – quick. So I did.

Then there we all are, standing in front of him, and I give him some wine to help with whatever it is (and no, I didn't take a drink first) when he tells us that he's had this vision: while he was praying an angel had come to him and told him that God was pleased with all he'd done, and that he was to send to Joppa for someone called Peter, who would help him. Well, I could see Marcus was all overcome – he and the master standing there with their mouths hanging open – amazed at this wonderful thing, and what it could all mean. But I'm standing there thinking Joppa! Nigh on 50 kilometres away – and just walk in and ask for someone named Peter! I mean, you know the place – as big as Caesarea. Cornelius had to be mad, or on something. Surely, I think, we'd better wait a bit and see if he changes his mind when he's had a sit-down and really thought it through. But no – we have to go now. Marcus is keen and even Kedar looks excited. Oh, and we have one more bit of information: this Peter is staying with someone called Simon, a tanner – now there's a help. So then the whole house is in an uproar as food and water are got ready, and everyone's talking about it – the angel and vision and everything – and then there we are – suddenly setting off on two days' hard walking, chasing a dream …

Once we're on the road I decide to make the most of the change, after all Kedar is a friend of mine and Marcus is all right for a Roman and at least gives us a bit of protection, and does find us somewhere reasonable at night. I talk it over with Kedar and discover he really believes we're going to find this Peter, reckons the master's vision was real and so God will help us. He argues with me about the gods – nothing new in that – we'd been arguing about faith a good while. I could see it helped some people accept their lot in life and some are better for it, but I've always thought there are too many priests and priestesses having a cushy life at other people's expense, and too many who use the gods to peddle their own views.

Anyway, we get to Joppa before midday, and I'm smiling to myself as we start asking for this 'Simon the tanner', and wondering how long it will be before Marcus gives up, and whether we'd get the night in Joppa before setting off back. I do my bit of asking around – and then someone does know a tanner called Simon and gives us directions. Marcus and Kedar go up on cloud nine and I'm a bit taken aback to tell the truth. Still, the chances of him having a guest called Peter have to be pretty remote. We walk through the streets and knock on the door and Marcus starts explaining, when this Jewish guy comes down the stairs from the roof – and not only is he Peter, but right at that moment he's been having a vision, in which he's been told we're coming for him, and what's more he's to come back with us. It's not just Marcus and Kedar who are overcome now – for once in my life I don't know what to think. I'm just, well – stunned. It's just a bit much to put down to coincidence. And I can't see how it could be a fix either, or why – and if there really is a God after all, I've got some serious thinking to do. So I listen: you can pick up a lot listening.

It's soon clear that Peter and Marcus have never met, nor did Peter know my master. In fact he wouldn't have wanted to because his people keep themselves to themselves and aren't too keen on the rest of us. But Peter has changed his mind about that because of the vision from God. Peter is one of these new Christians following the Way. He used to know Jesus, who got crucified when he challenged the priests. Except he still knows him somehow because it seems this Jesus rose from the dead. And Peter tells us more about him and I listen – I can't stop listening about Jesus …

All the way back I'm asking him questions, and he answers. Peter doesn't mind talking to a slave like this because in his mind I'm his brother. Marcus and Kedar join in, and I can see Kedar has that stupid grin on his face I want to knock off, but don't because this is too important. We are outside the master's house and Cornelius runs out to meet Peter and what's more goes down on his knees to him. Peter soon puts a stop to that. The master is beside himself with joy that Peter is real – has come – and what's more has entered his house. When they hear that Peter has had a vision too, and that we were part of it, there's even more joy and excitement – and then it happens …

I don't know how to describe it. It's difficult to put into words. We were listening to Peter telling us about Jesus, and the next moment it was like the room was full of something – an energy, the Spirit … I couldn't see it but it was all around, and I knew that it loved me … that God loved me. God's light was all around us – and we were praising God right from our hearts, in words I didn't know but somehow understood (no – I had not been drinking, nor had anyone else).

I said it was hard to explain, but I wish you had been there – because it was so amazing. Peter and his friends were so overcome to see us praising God like that, that they baptised us all there on the spot. So I'm a Christian now …The whole world seems different …

Prayer after Communion:

May we who have feasted at Christ's banquet
follow his dance into the unfamiliar places,
living gladly the dreams and visions
God sends for our world.
Amen

A reflection on the story
of the Transfiguration

Joy Mead

Six days later Jesus took Peter, James and John with him and led them up a high mountain by themselves. And in their presence he was transfigured; his clothes became dazzling white, with a whiteness no bleacher on earth could equal. They saw Elijah appear and Moses with him, talking with Jesus.

Mark 9:2–6 (REB)[1]

How good it is that we are here.
This is It. We have arrived.
We will put up tents and shelters
… chapels and churches.
Others arriving at this place
will see what we think we know,
see our attempt to pin him down.
Why should we move on?
Here we have found identity and meaning
in the incomprehensibility of things.
We will hold on to this experience
for dear life and human sanity.

But there is no holding on.
The cloud is upon us.
We are covered in shadow
and immobile with fear.
He dances ahead
transfigured in his suffering,
risen and free,
and we must let go.

What we thought we were here for
is only a shell,
a husk of meaning.
What we follow, watch, love,
interpret and attempt to contain
within our poverty of understanding
is no longer here.

The man, the moment, the meaning
go before – a light so bright
nothing could hold
or overcome it.
We can only follow,
leaving behind one mystery
to seek another mystery.
Each arrival is but a step further
in a continual exploration
which allows no settlement,
no pitching of tents, no making of shelters,
no protection of visions, no containment
of our individual experience.

There is only the pilgrimage
and discipleship, its meaning,
if it has meaning, in exploration.
What we have found
we cannot preserve.
What we still seek
is the warmer sun,
the transforming light
of creation,
the recognition of life:

the ever-new, ever-changing search
for what we have always known.

Source:

1. Scripture quotations taken from the Revised English Bible, copyright © Cambridge University Press and Oxford University Press 1989. All rights reserved.

Ruth's harvest

Worship resources for Harvest

Tim Aldred

Introduction

These resources are intended to be used together to help plan a harvest service. Alternatively, individual resources can be used or adapted as needed. The resources draw on the story of Ruth, Naomi, Orpah and Boaz in the Book of Ruth.

When I am stripped of power
When I am grieving
When I am a stranger
When I am humiliated

May I trust in your promised land
May I know your joy
May I meet you within and in others
May I learn that your harvest is for all

When I am powerful
When I am celebrating
When I am at home
When I am rewarded

May I trust in your promised land
May I know your joy
May I meet you within and in others
May I learn that your harvest is for all

Tim Aldred

A Harvest service (I)

Opening responses:

Holy Spirit of God,
WE INVITE YOU AMONG US.

As we come to celebrate your harvest
and to pray for your justice
WE ALSO ASK YOU TO BRING YOUR PEACE.

So that the quiet place inside us may speak.
IN STILLNESS MAY WE BE AT ONE WITH YOU.
AMEN

Silence

As we prepare for worship now,
our good lives can be tangled with thorns.
Thorns of failure and sadness.
Tangles of duties and demands.

LORD, CUT AWAY THE THORNS THAT WOUND AND CHOKE.
FREE US TO LIVE AND TO GROW IN YOUR LIGHT.

(A more formal confession/absolution can also be included here, if desired.)

Hymn/song

Prayer of thanksgiving:

God's world is an island of life and beauty –
formed of stardust, warmed by the sun.
Below us lies melting rock, above us stretches cold vacuum.
We live between: our home –
this thin strip of soil, water and air.

In which we share our lives together.
Which is alive with the Holy Spirit.

Upon which Jesus lived, died and rose again.
From which God's harvest comes.

GOD, WE THANK YOU FOR OUR HOME ON EARTH.
WE THANK YOU FOR OUR LIVES TOGETHER.
WE THANK YOU FOR YOUR LOVE AND CARE.
WE THANK YOU FOR THE HARVEST.

What is harvest?:

Voice 1:   What is harvest? Harvest is a time of hope:
           We have bread, warmth and shelter for tomorrow.

Voice 2:   What is harvest? Harvest is a time of fear:
           Our crops have failed, jobs are lost, a hard winter is to come.

Voice 1:   What is harvest? Harvest is a time of plenty:
           We receive with joy good gifts from God.

Voice 2:   What is harvest? Harvest is a time of empty shelves:
           We work the fields and factories but now go without.

Voice 1:   What is God's harvest? Plough the fields and scatter:
           a marrow on the altar and a tin of beans for charity?

Voice 2:   What is God's harvest? God's harvest is justice lived out with
           joy: food and fairness for today and tomorrow.

           FOR GOOD HARVESTS, WE BLESS YOU, LORD.
           WHERE HARVESTS FAIL, WE CRY OUT TO YOU, LORD.
           WHEN WE ARE FULL, INSPIRE US TO ACT.
           WHEN WE ARE EMPTY, FILL US WITH YOUR HOLY SPIRIT.

Bible readings: Choose one or more of the following: Ruth 1:8–18, Ruth 2:1–16, Ruth 3:1–11

A psalm said or sung (suggested Psalms: 8, 16, 19, 24, 65)

Drama: A harvest story: a drama (see part II)

Group work or a talk/reflection (see part III)

Hymn/song

Prayers of intercession:

Ruth, Naomi and Orpah were destitute, in need of refuge:
We pray for an end to poverty.
BRING US YOUR HARVEST OF JUSTICE AND PEACE.

Ruth was a foreigner, of the 'wrong' religion and race:
We pray for an end to war and the hatred that feeds it.
BRING US YOUR HARVEST OF JUSTICE AND PEACE.

Ruth, Naomi and Orpah were women, with fewer rights than men:
We pray for an end to discrimination and the violence it feeds.
BRING US YOUR HARVEST OF JUSTICE AND PEACE.

Boaz had power – land, money and authority:
We pray for all who hold power in our complex world.
BRING US YOUR HARVEST OF JUSTICE AND PEACE.

Ruth, Naomi and Orpah were grieving:
We pray for an end to suffering.
BRING US YOUR HARVEST OF JUSTICE AND PEACE.

Ruth found a home with Naomi and Boaz:
May we find community between us and a home with you.
BRING US YOUR HARVEST OF JUSTICE AND PEACE.

Alternative prayer of intercession:

Lord, just as Ruth did not seek charity but the right to harvest
we do not seek charity for our sisters and brothers who

grow the world's food
stitch the world's clothes
mine the world's metals
and yet remain poor.

We ask you for the justice of Boaz

in food and farming
in trade and finance
in human rights
in government and law

for women and men
for the natural world
and for children yet to be born.
WE ASK FOR YOUR JUSTICE LIVED OUT WITH JOY.
WE ASK FOR FAIRNESS WRITTEN ON OUR HEARTS,
THAT ALL MAY SEE A FAIRER WORLD.
AMEN

'God's harvest is ...' (period of open prayer):

Folk are invited to give their own examples of what God's harvest is about. For instance, 'God's harvest is justice and peace'; or 'God's harvest is an end to sadness' ... The leader could start this off.

After each statement, a sung response could be used (e.g. 'Through our lives and by our prayers', from Heaven Shall Not Wait, *John L. Bell and Graham Maule, Wild Goose Publications).*

The prayers conclude with the following response, or other suitable words:

LORD, WE LONG FOR YOUR HARVEST.
WE ARE READY TO WORK IN YOUR FIELDS,
BUT ONLY YOU CAN MAKE YOUR HARVEST GROW.
AMEN

Hymn/song: 'Blessed are the ones I call the poor', from *Heaven Shall Not Wait*, John L. Bell and Graham Maule, Wild Goose Publications; or 'Christ be our light', by Bernadette Farrell, from CH4

(If this liturgy is to be used as part of a communion service, the communion liturgy can be included here.)

Prayer of commitment:

We commit ourselves to the service of God and all his people in the words that Ruth said to Naomi (Ruth 1:16, NIV):

WHERE YOU GO, I WILL GO.
WHERE YOU STAY, I WILL STAY.
YOUR PEOPLE WILL BE MY PEOPLE.
AMEN

Alternative prayer of commitment:

WHEN I AM STRIPPED OF POWER
WHEN I AM GRIEVING
WHEN I AM A STRANGER
WHEN I AM HUMILIATED

MAY I TRUST IN YOUR PROMISED LAND
MAY I KNOW YOUR JOY
MAY I MEET YOU WITHIN AND IN OTHERS
MAY I LEARN THAT YOUR HARVEST IS FOR ALL

WHEN I AM POWERFUL
WHEN I AM CELEBRATING
WHEN I AM AT HOME
WHEN I AM REWARDED

MAY I TRUST IN YOUR PROMISED LAND
MAY I KNOW YOUR JOY
MAY I MEET YOU WITHIN AND IN OTHERS
MAY I LEARN THAT YOUR HARVEST IS FOR ALL

Blessing:

Holy Spirit of God,
may the space within that we keep for you
become ever deeper and wider.
May the busyness of our brains
and the cares of our hearts
give way to the light of your presence.

O GOD, COME HOME WITH US THIS HARVEST TIME
AND EVERMORE
AMEN

A Harvest story: a drama (II)

This drama, based on the Book of Ruth, can be acted straight through, or the different chapters of the story could be interspersed throughout a service or a workshop.

Boaz: a man of means
Naomi: an older widow
Ruth: a young foreign widow

A village near Bethlehem, over three thousand years ago …

Chapter 1

Boaz: I'm starting the harvest tomorrow. I've got large fields, so I've hired in men to help out. The barley looks good! I'll be fine for the winter, and I'll have plenty to sell.

Naomi: Naomi means 'beautiful' – did you know that? Can you believe it? I was beautiful once, I suppose, but then my man died, and then my sons. Me and their barren, heathen widows left to fend for ourselves. Crawling back here to our old shack with my tail between my legs, and an enemy heathen in tow – yes, I know what they say in the village. 'Bitter' is more like it. Yes, call me 'Bitter', that's a better name.

Ruth: She didn't want me to come, she made that clear. But where would I go? Back to my parents? Another mouth to feed; soiled goods for the marriage market. Besides, I made my vow. She is my mother now, and I am her daughter.

Chapter 2, part 1

Boaz: The sun is up, the grain is ripe. A good choice for a harvest day!

Naomi: I've got our old plot, but it's overgrown with thorns. No time to plant a crop before harvest, even if I had money for seed. If we're to get through winter I'll have to sell up. There's no choice.

Ruth: Naomi says the poor can take what the reapers leave behind – I must do it, I'm young, I can work. But I'm afraid of the men. I've seen the way they look at me; I've heard the cat calls: fair game, they're thinking. But no harvesting, no food. There's no choice.

Chapter 2, part 2

Boaz: I've heard about this one at the tavern – I should have guessed Naomi would send her to glean. She's got some guts, that one, doing her duty by Naomi, coming right into the lion's den – no way back to her people now. Not much welcome for foreigners round here; memories are long.

Ruth: He warned off the labourers who were eyeing me up, and let me work in safety with the women. He let me share the food at lunchtime, and even called on his God – my God now, I suppose – to bless me. But something else happened today. Just for a moment, I didn't feel like a foreigner.

Naomi: She was gone so long … from dawn till dusk she was gone. But she came back with thirteen kilos of barley! Enough to keep us both for a few weeks. But this hand-to-mouth life is no life. Is this our lot until we die?

Chapter 3

Boaz: All is safely gathered in! And a good party with the lads to celebrate. They need to let off some steam I guess. What happens on the threshing floor stays on the threshing floor ...

Ruth: I don't want to go to the threshing floor. I know what it makes me look like. A young widow coming in the night to where the men are sleeping off the booze.

Naomi: It is a risk, and hard on Ruth. But I have to make a hard choice. We can't live on handouts much longer.

Chapter 4

Reflectively, looking back after a period of time ...

Ruth: I know now that Naomi should have gone to plead our cause: he's her relative, his duty was to her. Naomi told me to give myself to him there and then, but when he woke, I couldn't do it.

Boaz: I knew what she had come for. Or, I thought I did. But I was wrong. She asked for her rights. She claimed her rights to protection under God's law. I'd given her charity before, but now she asked for justice.

Naomi: I thought all men were the same. But I had misjudged him – he did his duty and more.

Ruth: He did not begrudge us justice, but delivered it with joy and wedded it to kindness.

Boaz: That was the harvest: that God brought me a new family.

Naomi: That was the harvest: that God reconciled me to my people.

Ruth: That was the harvest: that God welcomed me to a new home.

Notes for group work or a talk (III)

These notes can be used for group work during the service or with a small study group. They could also be used as ideas for a short talk or sermon.

If planning group work as part of a service: Ask the congregation to form into small groups, with each group looking at one or two questions each. After 5-10 minutes discussion, a spokesperson from each group shares the top one or two insights from the discussion with the rest of the congregation. Each group can also record important points on pieces of card or Post-it notes, which are then fixed to a display board for everyone to see. Some of the questions give the opportunity for people to share personal experiences – but it is important to say that no one should feel under pressure to do so.

Finally, ask groups to spend a few minutes discussing the action that God may call us to in response. These could be practical responses such as political action, supporting campaigns or choices about the use of our time or money. Responses might also involve a commitment to address attitudes that harm or stigmatise vulnerable or marginalised people. Folk may also be called to respond in prayer.

Question 1: structural injustice and women

Naomi and her daughters-in-law, Orpah and Ruth, face particular problems because of their gender. They become destitute when their husbands die (Ruth chapter 1). Ruth works from dawn to dusk in the fields, acts with godly integrity and courage throughout and proves herself 'better than seven sons' (Ruth chapter 4). Despite this, she remains subject to decisions taken by Boaz and the other town elders about her marriage and Naomi's property.

Women still face structural injustices. According to the Fairtrade Foundation, women in Africa grow 80% of the staple food, but own only 1% of the land. In Britain, only 23% of Members of Parliament are women.

How does God call us to respond to the injustices faced by women, whether women close to us or in wider society?

Question 2: the things that keep people poor

There is, theoretically, some protection offered to Naomi and Ruth under Mosaic law. They have the right to glean leftover grain from the harvest. But whether or not this right will be met depends on the integrity of wealthy landowners like Boaz. Boaz goes beyond his legal duty: by inviting Ruth to eat with his workers; and by asking for God's blessing on her he treats her in the same way as a member of his household (Ruth chapter 2).

Ruth collected an exceptional amount of grain on that first day – enough to feed Naomi and herself for perhaps 3 or 4 weeks, if used carefully. Even so, Ruth would have struggled to collect enough grain during the harvest to see Naomi and herself through the winter. The right to glean gave emergency help to Ruth and Naomi, but did not offer them a long-term way out.

What things can stand in the way of treating people in need with dignity and respect? How can we go beyond charity to understand – and change – the things that keep people poor?

Question 3: the poor and vulnerable

Both Boaz and Naomi show concern that Ruth could be assaulted when she goes to work alone in the fields. She is especially vulnerable, because she is a single, foreign woman from the enemy Moabite tribe. Her poverty means that she has no choice but to do work that puts her at risk (Ruth chapter 2).

Poverty can place people in impossible positions. Nyasha (not her real name) is a sex worker who lives in Zimbabwe. Interviewed by the charity Progressio, she said: *'Because of a lack of money with which to feed my family I got into sex work. It was a very difficult decision for me to make, because I am a Christian. But I felt I had no choices left. I just had to get money to support my children.'* [1]

People living in poverty have very few choices. They may take action that carries serious risk, or which leads to social stigma. What does this mean for the approach needed when working to tackle poverty?

Question 4: the rights of the poor

When Ruth asks Boaz to be a 'guardian redeemer', she is claiming her rights to protection under Mosaic law. Boaz buys Naomi's land and brings her and Ruth into his household. Under the law, the land will be returned to Ruth's descendants in the year of Jubilee. The nearest relative to Naomi refuses to meet this duty, because he doesn't want to risk his children's inheritance. Boaz, by contrast, accepts it gladly (Ruth chapters 3 and 4).

Are the rights of poor people to receive fair treatment met gladly today, or only when it suits?

Question 5: taking action

Ruth, Naomi and Boaz may be acting for a mixture of reasons at different times in the story. We can see the simple force of circumstances and poverty, the calls of duty and responsibility, and impressive demonstrations of love and compassion. The references to God in Ruth also show that both Ruth and Boaz link their actions to their faith.

When you have responded to need or injustice, what inspired or motivated you? At times when you have faced difficulties yourself, what kind of support did you need or value?

Notes and sources:

1. From Progressio. Used by permission of Progressio. Progressio is an international development charity working for justice and the eradication of poverty: www. progressio.org.uk

Live in the light

Reflections on peacemaking and reconciliation

Ruth Harvey

Introduction

> *'Be patterns, be examples in all countries, places, islands, nations, wherever you come, that your carriage and life may preach among all sorts of people, and to them; then you will come to walk cheerfully over the world, answering that of God in everyone.'*

– George Fox, 1656, from *Advices & Queries*

Advices & Queries is a summary of the wisdom of the Yearly Meeting of the Religious Society of Friends (Quakers) in Britain. *'A reminder of the insights of the Society'*, these A&Q have been gathered and modified through experience since the late seventeenth century. Within their 42 brief paragraphs, they offer guidance for the individual worshipper, for the community of believers and for each of us all alone and in community as we engage in the concerns for peace, justice, equality, simplicity and right relationship in the world.

In the following five reflections I have selected excerpts that 'speak to my condition' in the hope that they may also 'speak' to yours (and have suggested further paragraphs that may also be useful). I have followed the pattern of beginning with inner reconciliation, moving through reconciliation in our worshipping community or church, to reconciliation in the world. For a complete (free) copy of *Advices & Queries* visit www.quaker.org.uk.

1. Inwardly reconciled: 'Cherish that of God within you'

> *'Bring the whole of your life under the ordering of the spirit of Christ. Are you open to the healing power of God's love? Cherish that of God within you, so that this love may grow in you and guide you. Let your worship and your daily life enrich each other. Treasure your experience of God, however it comes to you. Remember that Christianity is not a notion but a way.'*
>
> (*Advices & Queries* 2. See also 1, 3, 4, 7, 11, 28, 31 and 32)

Being a 'reconciled reconciler' is a lifelong journey – first we are invited to be reconciled with ourselves – with all those parts of our self we struggle to embrace, those character traits that we perhaps even deny, or push away.

The God of love loves each part of us, for God is within and without.

To be a healer, it helps to know how it feels to be in need of healing. To be a peacemaker, it helps to know how it feels to be at war with oneself. To be a reconciler, it helps to know how it feels to be reconciled to oneself. To love our neighbour as we love ourselves, first we must know what it means to love our self from the inside out.

In so much of Christendom it may seem counter-cultural to focus on the self, to be mindful of the peace that Christ wishes for each one of us. But Jesus spoke of living in the present, of embracing the kingdom, present now within each one of us.

- *What is the 'note'[1] that resonates most deeply within you?*

- *When, and in what contexts, do you feel unquestionably cherished by God? Notice these times. Nurture, welcome and encourage them. For it is out of this space of inner peace that we are more able to become peacemakers in the world.*

2. Resilient and calm: 'Live adventurously'

> *'Live adventurously. When choices arise, do you take the way that offers the fullest opportunity for the use of your gifts in the service of God and the community? Let your life speak. When decisions have to be made, are you ready to join with others in seeking clearness, asking for God's guidance and offering counsel to one another?'*
>
> (*Advices & Queries 27*. See also 28, 41)

With the children in our local Quaker meeting we explored what it might mean to *'live adventurously'*. For some, this meant planning and taking trips to wild parts of the country. For others, living adventurously meant standing up to school bullies, speaking 'truth to power', coming forward with ideas rather than holding back. Yet others reflected that to live adventurously would mean to give up busyness. Comfort in activity can mask a deeper discomfort in stillness. To stop, seek out stillness in busy lives may lead us on an inner adventure.

Margaret Silf, in her book *Inner Compass* (Loyola Press), offers a simple, Ignatius-inspired exercise for discerning how to live adventurously. She invites us first to reflect on *'the givens'* in our lives, those things that we cannot change: perhaps our genetics, the place and time of our birth … After reflecting on these, then try to set them to one side. Next, she invites us to reflect on those areas of life over which we have choice: maybe work, location, use of time … and then to set these aside. Finally, she invites us to reflect on what remains: the core, the inner identity, who we are at root once the outer layers of happenstance and choice have been set aside for a while. She suggests that it is out of this inner 'I am' that we encounter the immanent God, the God who dwells within. And from this inner place of clarity, the 'God-seed' can grow and flourish – and we can then 'live adventurously' in the world. This, I think, is the 'clearness' of which Quakers speak: an inner clarity that speaks through the everyday.

- *What does 'live adventurously' mean to you?*

- *How do you seek God's guidance in your decisions?*

- *How open are you to any surprise that may emerge as you wait?*

- *What comfort zones do you inhabit?*

- *What could nudge you out of familiar patterns?*

3. Reconciliation in community: 'Think it possible that you may be mistaken'

> *'Do you respect that of God in everyone though it may be expressed in unfamiliar ways or be difficult to discern? Each of us has a particular experience of God and each must find the way to be true to it. When words are strange or disturbing to you, try to sense where they come from and what has nourished the lives of others. Listen patiently and seek the truth which other people's opinions may contain for you. Avoid hurtful criticism and provocative language. Do not allow the strength of your convictions to betray you into making statements or allegations that are unfair or untrue. Think it possible that you may be mistaken.'*

(*Advices & Queries* 17. See also 22 and 26)

Dear Lord,
we pray for a round table[2] –
    a United Nations negotiating table;
    a Number 10 oval office table;
    a communion kitchen table –
    any such sacramental table.
A table where the corners have been replaced by curves,
and where the stuff (and word) of life is blessed and sent around
    (like salt and spice),
where the Holy Spirit loops the bend to rest –
these are holy round tables:
places of reconciliation.

For reconciliation
to come around,
give us grace, good Lord,

    to notice our stolid square-ness;
then so much more grace
to embrace the complete 'round' in ourselves.

Where rough edges
    have been smoothed,
where hard opinions
    have been softened,
we give you thanks that
here
is the space

for reconciling love.

Amen

4. Peace in the church

> *'Take time to learn about other people's experience of the Light.'*
>
> (Extract from *Advices & Queries* 5. See also 6, 14, 18 and 22)

It was a warm summer's day and we were resting from our work. A team from across Europe had joined together for a summer language school, while also building a new sauna for the local community (*'a demanding common task alone builds community,'* I hear George MacLeod saying in the background). Living in a hut on the White Plains of eastern Poland, not far from the border with Russia, we were a mixed bag of trainee theologians: Baptists, Orthodox, Presbyterians, Catholics and Methodists, all in our 20s. Over the evening campfire, talk turned to belief, theology and eventually to baptism. And in the heat of the flames, and conversation, I found myself arguing my line of thought fiercely. In a lull, I realised I was arguing for a concept about which I really knew very little. I was taking time to push my line, rather than to learn about my friends' *'experience of the Light'*. That was a turning point for me, after which I realised that to live out my passion for unity I had to be prepared to set aside my own beliefs for a while in order to hear those of others.

In Place for Hope *(www.placeforhope.org.uk)* we support people of faith, many in local churches, as they transform conflict and embrace difference. Working with groups, we initially agree ways to ensure that our gathering will be effective. These are agreements to which we will hold one another in the course of our work. They can act as a steady rock while all else may seem fluid. One of these agreements is that we will listen to 'one voice at a time'. This means that when one person is speaking, others listen. Full attention is given to the speaker. This also means 'stilling the voice in our head'. There may be no one else speaking, but the voice in our head may be rehearsing a response, a reaction, a refute to what is being said.

- As we search for peace and (comm)unity in the church, are we prepared to sit lightly to what we hold dear in order to understand more fully the Light of the other?

- In our search for unity among believers, to what extent are we looking for community, or for uniformity?

5. Peace in the world

> *'Bring into God's light those emotions, attitudes and prejudices in yourself which lie at the root of destructive conflict, acknowledging your need for forgiveness and grace. In what ways are you involved in the work of reconciliation between individuals, groups and nations?'*
>
> (*Advices & Queries* 32. See also 33, 34, 35, 36 and 42)

The Truth and Reconciliation Commissions of Rwanda, Northern Ireland, Liberia and South Africa remind us that many great hearts and minds have, over decades, worked tirelessly for reconciliation through attentive listening, forgiveness and the grace of God. The Forgiveness Project, Forgiveness Challenge, and the Elders (Mary Robinson, Desmond Tutu, Kofi Annan and others) remind us that many great people are still putting their energies into this task of peace and reconciliation.[3]

We can all be agents of change, or 'global elders', in the sense that we are, each one of us, called by God to be peacemakers in the world.

In the Quaker tradition, an elder is someone who is *'responsible for fostering the spiritual life of the meeting'*. In other traditions, elders are *'men and women called and committed to ... help release, realise and enrich the full Christian potential implicit in the spiritual calling of all those in the Church and, indeed, in the wider society they encounter in everyday life'*.[4]

- In what ways are you a global elder in your own community?

- What does forgiveness mean to you? Share a story of a powerful experience of either giving or receiving forgiveness.

Notes and sources:

1. John Knox spoke of *'the notes of Presbyterianism'*: the core, resonating identities that give that tradition its singularity.

2. Inspired by 'A Round Table Church', by Chuck Lathrop, in *Seasons with the Spirit*, Ruth Harvey (Ed.), CTBI Publications

3. See http://theforgivenessproject.com, www.forgivenesschallenge.com/, http://theelders.org/

4. *The Eldership Past and Present,* the Eldership Working Party of the Church of Scotland, 2003

Unexpected blessings

A dialogue and reflection
on Genesis 18:1-15

Dave Broom

Introduction

Voice: Our reading *(today/tonight)* comes from Genesis 18 [1–15]. The desert is an inhospitable, potentially deadly environment for human beings. Temperatures can rise to 45 degrees Celsius, or more, in the daytime, and plunge to as low as minus 18 at night. There is the risk of dehydration, heatstroke and frostbite and the danger of sandstorms.

Desert-dwellers know the essential basic importance of shelter, food and water. And it is customary for them to offer hospitality to those who pass by their tents on their travels. Hospitality is a sacred act, and one that is vital if people are to survive in the harsh conditions.

This giving seems to be all one way but, as we shall see in our story, can sometimes lead to unexpected blessings ...

Reader: The Lord appeared to Abraham at the sacred trees of Mamre. As Abraham was sitting at the entrance of his tent during the hottest part of the day, he looked up and saw three men standing there. As soon as he saw them, he ran out to meet them. Bowing down with his face touching the ground, he said, 'Sirs, please do not pass by my home without stopping; I am here to serve you. Let me bring some water for you to wash your feet; you can rest here beneath this tree. I will also bring a bit of food; it will give you strength to continue your journey. You have honoured me by coming to my home, so let me serve you.' They replied, 'Thank you; we accept.' Abraham hurried into the tent and said to Sarah, 'Quick, take a sack of your best flour, and bake some bread.' Then he ran to the herd and picked out a calf that was tender and fat, and gave it to a servant, who hurried to get it ready. He took some cream, some milk, and the meat, and set the food before the men. There under the tree he served them himself, and they ate.

Then they asked him, 'Where is your wife Sarah?' 'She is there in the tent,' he answered. One of them said, 'Nine months from now I will come back, and your wife Sarah will have a son.'

Voice: Abraham had some very unexpected guests: guests who brought him some very good – and unexpected – news. Abraham offered self-giving hospitality to his guests, and his guests rewarded him.

Would we receive unexpected visitors in the same way today? ...

Scene: Israel's Household and Garden Supplies, Peckham, South London

Dramatis personae:

Mr Israel/Abe – shop owner
Sarah – Abe's wife
Ronald – a young shop assistant

Sound effect: Rain (use a rain stick or a recording), gradually fade ...

This dialogue/drama can be spoken, or acted out in the crossing of a church, etc. Be creative, have fun and adapt this to your situation.

Narrator: Peckham, London, November 2016 ... It seems to be raining all over London. The streets are dark and cold. It's the end of the day and people are hurrying home from work. Mr Israel, the elderly owner of Israel's Household and Garden Supplies, is sitting in the back of his shop doing the accounts for the week. His wife, Sarah, is also in the back room, talking to a friend on the phone, even though, throughout the 35 years of their marriage, he has constantly told her *not* to talk on the telephone while he is doing the accounts. There are no customers in the shop and Ronald, the young shop assistant, is standing behind the counter staring into space after a long busy day, when he suddenly notices something ...

Ronald: (anxious) Mr Israel, Mr Israel –

Mr Israel: (annoyed) Ronald, I'm in here. Come and find me if you want to talk to me.

Sarah: *(talking on telephone)* Ooh, I know, I saw her yesterday, all dressed up, nowhere to go, looking like butter wouldn't melt …

Ronald: *(loudly)* Mr Israel –

Mr Israel: Will you please be quiet! I'm trying to finish the books. And Sarah, for the last time, will you please go and take that phone call somewhere else?

Sarah: Mind, there's some would say she had something going on with that new vicar … You know, the one who looks like Clark Gable … *(Pause)* … Ooh, I know!

Ronald: *(bursting into room)* Mr Israel!

Mr Israel: Oh, for goodness' sake – what is it?

Ronald: There's three men standing out in the road!

Mr Israel: There *are* three men, Ronald. There *are* … And anyway, what's that got to do with me? It's a free country. People are entitled to stand in the road if they want to … even in the pouring rain. We are a shop, Ronald: we do need to attract customers. Some people have been known to call that business.

Ronald: But, they're big men. And they're right outside.

Sarah: *(putting down the phone)* Ooh, maybe you'd better go and have a look, Abe. Might be trouble.

Mr Israel: *(less confident)* Erm, yeah, yeah, maybe I should. When you say 'big'. How big exactly?

Ronald: Well, massive!

Mr Israel: Massive?

Ronald: Yeah, and they've got wings.

Mr Israel: Wings?! Ronald, have you been drinking the cooking sherry again? I've warned you about that, my lad.

Ronald: No, honestly, Mr Israel. Not a drop, and they do have wings.

Sarah: *(looking out the window)* He's right, you know, Abe, they do have wings. They're very serious though. And the one on the left is kind of cute. *(Waving)* Woo-hoo!

Mr Israel: Sarah, come away from there. Stop making a scene.

Sarah: Oh Abe, they look all wet and cold standing out there. Go and see what they want. Invite them in for a cup of tea.

Mr Israel: A cup of tea?! Heavens woman, whatever next? They could be anyone. Do you want me to get stabbed?

Sarah: Oh, they don't look the stabbing sort. They look nice. I'll go and put the kettle on. We've got some of those new biscuits the McVitie's rep brought round. I'll get them out.

Mr Israel: Tea? Biscuits? Big men standing outside my shop – with wings? Has the world gone mad?

Ronald: *(sounding mystical)* They might be messengers …

Mr Israel: Eh?

Ronald: You know, from outer space, like *The X-Files*. Aliens come to give us esoteric knowledge.

Mr Israel: 'Esoteric knowledge!' You'll be getting an esoteric clip round the ear in a minute, Ronald, my boy. There are no aliens, nor ghosts, nor Loch Ness monsters for that matter. There's a perfectly logical explanation to all this. It's probably some sort of stag night stunt.

Ronald: But those wings look real.

Sarah: Ooh, they do, Abe. Doesn't look like a costume.

Abe: Oh, for goodness' sake! Am I the only sane person in this room? I'll go and see what they want.
            (Pause)

Mr Israel: *(opening the shop door, speaking slowly)* Hello, gentlemen ... Yes, I'm Abraham Israel ... Yes, my wife is Sarah ... No, no, I have no son ... Oh, I see ... Erm, Sarah has the kettle on ... Would you like to come in for tea? ...

Reflection

Sometimes we find God in the most unlikely situations and in the most unlikely people. But often we miss God through being too busy or being unwilling to open ourselves to possibility and the moment. Hebrews 13:2 says: 'Do not neglect to show hospitality to strangers: for by doing so some have entertained angels unawares.'

Who was the last unexpected visitor you entertained? Did they bring good news? Were you happy to see them, or were you busy doing something else? Did your visitor bring you any unexpected blessings? ...

Source:

The Prodigal Son returns to Peckham

A dialogue, activity and reflection on Luke 15:11-32

Dave Broom

Dialogue

Narrator: A reading from the Gospel according to St Luke [15:11–32]. Listen now, for God speaks to us in surprising ways ...

Reader: Jesus said: 'There was a man who had two sons. The younger one said to his father, "Father, give me my share of the estate." So he divided his property between them. Not long after that, the younger son got together all he had, set off for a distant country and there squandered his wealth in wild living. After he had spent everything, there was a severe famine in that whole country, and he began to be in need. So he went and hired himself out to a citizen of that country, who sent him to his fields to feed pigs. He longed to fill his stomach with the pods that the pigs were eating, but no one gave him anything ...

Narrator: The scene is a pub in Peckham, South London. It's early evening and people are just coming in after work. The landlord is standing at the bar polishing glasses as one of the regulars walks in.

Landlord: Evening, Pete. Usual?

Pete: Thanks, Ian, don't mind if I do. Don't mind if I do! Did you see the game Saturday? Shocking! They'll be relegated if this goes on. Need to go back to playing 4-4-2, if you ask me ...

Landlord: Never mind all that! Have you heard the latest? Terry's son Paul has come back.

Pete: What, the one that ran off with all his money? I thought he was a big shot in Ibiza! Owned that club all those top DJs and supermodels and footballers used to go to.

Landlord: No, the market crashed, didn't it. All went pear-shaped – he lost the lot! Not a penny to bless himself with! Just had the clothes he stood up in. Blagged his way onto a flight somehow and got back to London.

Reader: When he came to his senses, he said, "How many of my father's hired servants have food to spare, and here I am starving to

death! I will set out and go back to my father and say to him:
'Father, I have sinned against heaven and against you. I am no
longer worthy to be called your son; make me like one of your
hired servants.'" So he got up and went to his father …

Pete: I'm surprised he had the nerve to come back. Wouldn't want to
be showing my face around here after that. I bet Terry gave him
a right hiding.

Landlord: Not at all! He's welcomed him back with open arms. You should
go round there – it's like a week-long party. The neighbours had
to get the police round last night to do something about the
noise!

Reader: But while he was still a long way off, his father saw him and was
filled with compassion for him; he ran to his son, threw his arms
around him and kissed him. The son said to him, "Father, I have
sinned against heaven and against you. I am no longer worthy
to be called your son." But the father said to his servants,
"Quick! Bring the best robe and put it on him. Put a ring on his
finger and sandals on his feet. Bring the fattened calf and kill it.
Let's have a feast and celebrate. For this son of mine was dead
and is alive again; he was lost and is found." So they began to
celebrate …

Pete: What? Has Terry got religion or something? Paul nicked all his
money! I mean, Terry had been made redundant. Paul nicked
the redundancy payout. Terry had nothing. Poor bloke's been
having to work down Tesco's just to make ends meet.

Landlord: He's got his other son who's been helping out.

Pete: Yeah, well Darren's a good bloke. I know him from the darts
team. He wouldn't leave his old man high and dry like that.

Reader: Meanwhile, the older son was in the field. When he came near
the house, he heard music and dancing. So he called one of the
servants and asked him what was going on. "Your brother has
come," he replied, "and your father has killed the fattened calf
because he has him back safe and sound." …

Pete: But how does Darren feel about it? He can't have been glad to see Paul back again!

Landlord: He wasn't!

Reader: The older brother became angry and refused to go in. So his father went out and pleaded with him. But he answered his father, "Look! All these years I've been slaving for you and never disobeyed your orders. Yet you never gave me even a young goat so I could celebrate with my friends. But when this son of yours who has squandered your property with prostitutes comes home, you kill the fattened calf for him!" ...

Pete: I mean, how would you feel?! Darren's been helping his old man out all this time, supporting him, making sure he's OK. And Paul waltzes back in without a 'by your leave' and it's like Darren doesn't exist. It's well out of order!

Landlord: That's family for you though, isn't it? You never give up on your kids. And it's not as though Darren's had a terrible time: Terry's always been there for him.

Reader: "My son," the father said, "you are always with me, and everything I have is yours. But we had to celebrate and be glad, because this brother of yours was dead and is alive again; he was lost and is found."'

Landlord: The thing is, Pete, Terry's love for Paul is unconditional. He knows what a mess Paul is and he knows how sorry he is for messing up so badly. At the end of the day, despite everything, he's just glad to get Paul back ... Do you know, there's a story in the Bible a bit like this.

Pete: What – you got religion too? Blimey! What's going on around here?

Landlord: No, put a sock in it, Pete – and listen, you might learn something ... 'You see, there was once a man who had two sons, and the younger one said to his father, "Father, give me my share of the estate." So he divided his property between them ...' *(fade)*

Song

'I will arise', from *One Is the Body: Songs of Unity & Diversity*, John L. Bell, Wild Goose Publications

Activity

Which person in the Parable of the Prodigal Son do you identify with most, feel the most sympathy for?

Maybe the Prodigal Son?: He thought he had it made – living the high life with his parties, supermodels and footballer friends. But it proved to be a house built on sand. When the money was gone he had nothing.

Or perhaps the father?: who never gave up hope, waiting for his son and watching for a sign of his return; then forgiving his wayward son unconditionally and throwing a big party to celebrate his return.

Or maybe the older brother?: He'd worked hard all his life. He'd supported his father and had always been obedient, yet his father had never given him even a small amount so that he could have a party with his friends. And then suddenly his irritating, wilful brother reappears on the scene and everything is lavished on him.

In groups of 4 or 5, talk about which character you identify with, feel most sympathy for …

Reflection

In thinking about this story we probably find that we identify most with the older brother: 'How dare my younger brother just waltz back in here after everything he's done! I've been here all the time and what have I got to show for it?'

But God's ways are not our ways. Look again. William Barclay says that this parable should be called 'the Parable of the Loving Father'. The father completely accepts both his sons. He knows what they're like and he loves them both. Despite everything his younger son has done, he's waiting for him to come home. And he isn't just waiting – he runs to meet him when he's still on the way.

Jesus is telling us that God is like that: God's forgiveness is unconditional; there are no recriminations. We're not forgiven as a favour, as we humans might forgive each other. And there's no underlying hint that our sin may have been 'forgiven' … but can still be dragged up again if someone needs ammunition against us and be held as an ever-present threat. That isn't really forgiveness.

I feel a considerable sense of relief when reading this story. Maybe you do too. Jesus is telling us that however much we might mess up – and we all know that we do – God is not just waiting for us to come back home – but positively running towards us, holding the robe of honour, the ring of authority and the shoes of a beloved child of God.

Source:

Called to be an innkeeper

A reflection on Luke 10:25-37, the Good Samaritan

Elaine Gisbourne

I bring you my wounded ones:
the beaten, broken and messy,
the weary, the traumatised,
precious, wounded ones.

I bring to you the ones from whom
others turned their gaze,
out of fear, disgust, shame;
rejected when most vulnerable,
I bring them to you.

I bring them to you because I trust you.
To see beyond the blood and dirt,
to look deeper than the bruises and scars,
and hold them,
stay with them,
attend to them and care for them.

I know this work will cost you,
cost you more than you think you can give,
but I know you:
you will give to them from the depths of your own generosity,
and you will continue to hold them
until I return and set them on their way.

I trust you because I know you,
that my promise is enough for you,
and that you know it is our love which heals.

Jesus was a refugee

Resources for worship

Tom Gordon

Evacuated

'The high mountains are for the wild goats;
the rocks are a refuge for the badgers.'
Psalm 104:18 (RSV)

The Psalmist of old may be right. The high mountains with their rocks, caves and crevices may be ideally suited to provide refuge for goats and badgers and a host of other wild animals. But what of people who seek refuge, when even the roughest places are out of reach? What of our modern-day refugees, who seek shelter and warmth, who yearn for community and security, who long to be settled and live in peace? They are, surely, worth more of our attention than the animals of the wild who seem to be well enough equipped with refuge in their rocks and high mountains.

I read recently an account of a Syrian refugee family who had been provided with a basic tent by an aid agency, only to experience – battered by a storm and beaten upon by torrential rain – the tent collapsing around them, leaving them more vulnerable, frightened and confused than they had been before.

It was a symbol – our tent collapsing in the rain.

Our country, battered by the storm of violence and war;
our homes, destroyed by mortars and air-strikes;
our settled peace, swept away despite our prayers and pleadings;
our evacuation, enforced and frighteningly sudden;
our hopes and dreams, thrown into the mud in an untimely destruction.

Yet, this was more than a mere symbol.
It was our grim truth, our living certainty,
where country and home and peace and security are swept away,
and everything collapses;
when evacuation is the only option,
and we are refugees again.

It was a symbol – our tent collapsing in the rain –
but it was also our hellish reality,
the truth of our living.

It was a symbol – when we pitched our tent again.

The tent going up was another chance;
the trench around it was our protective moat;
the promise of a tin hut gave purpose to our dreams;
the new place was our hope of being settled for a while;
and heating, more than blankets, was our promise of salvation.

Yet, this was more than a mere symbol.
It was our hopeful truth, the creation of our potential …
Where the smallest of new beginnings is a statement of intent,
and building a future is a possibility once more;
when being settled offers different options,
and we are no longer labelled as refugees
but know ourselves as people with a home.

It was a symbol – when we pitched our tent again –
but it was also the reality we believe in,
the truth of our living hope.

The United Nations High Commissioner for Refugees (UNHCR)

Part of the mission of the UNHCR, as outlined in its 'Mission Statement', is described as follows:

'The United Nations High Commissioner for Refugees (UNHCR) is mandated by the United Nations to lead and coordinate international action for the worldwide protection of refugees and the resolution of refugee problems.

UNHCR's primary purpose is to safeguard the rights and well-being of refugees. UNHCR strives to ensure that everyone can exercise the right to seek asylum and find safe refuge in another state, or to return home voluntarily. By assisting refugees to return to their own country or to settle in another country, UNHCR also seeks lasting solutions to their plight …' [1]

A prayer for the UNHCR

Today I pray for the values and goals of the UNHCR ...

For the people who do their work
and those who benefit from it ...

For the places they serve
and the places where people wish they did ...

For the governments who offer support
and forgiveness for those who don't ...

For tribes and clans and peoples, humanity in all its glorious variety
and every broken and frightened individual ...

For the travellers and the settlers ...

For the fearful and the broken ...

For the stateless and those terrorised by their own state ...

For the givers and the receivers ...

For the whole and the broken ...

For resolution, for reconciliation and for peace ...

The Bible and refugees

The Bible tells of the history of the Jewish people and the birth of Christianity. After the Israelites are delivered from slavery in Egypt, God gives them the Law to govern their lives. The most familiar of over 600 regulations for life are the Ten Commandments. But there is one holy law, in the midst of all the rest, which has a particular influence in the context of how we respond to the refugee issue in our modern day. In the Book of Leviticus, chapter 19, verses 33–34, we read (from the New International Bible):

'When a foreigner resides among you in your land, do not ill-treat them. The foreigner residing among you must be treated as your native-born. Love them as yourself, for you were foreigners in Egypt. I am the Lord your God.'

Enshrined in the Law, therefore, is the instruction to show compassion to refugees. The Israelites had been refugees themselves, enslaved during their time in Egypt. In time they would experience exile in Babylon. So from the infancy of their nation, a people and their religion are defined by compassion towards aliens, strangers and refugees.

Jesus was a refugee

In marking World Refugee Day in 2014, Pope Francis made a moving appeal on behalf of the world's refugees – reminding his hearers that Jesus, too, was a refugee. He said:

'We believe that Jesus was a refugee, had to flee to save his life, with Saint Joseph and Mary, had to leave for Egypt ... Let us pray to Our Lady who knows the pain of refugees ...'

This being so, it's not surprising that Jesus, knowing for himself what refugee status was like, followed the injunction to show compassion to the needy, the stranger and the refugee that was fundamental to his Jewish upbringing. When the crowds asked him, at the start of his ministry: 'Then what shall we do?', he answered: 'The man who has two tunics is to share with him who has none; and he who has food is to do likewise.' (Luke 3:11, New American Standard Bible).

A prayer to my human Christ

In your infancy, you knew nothing ...
nothing of pain and terror,
nothing of uncertainty and danger,
nothing of fear and confusion,
nothing of loneliness and death.

That was for your mother to know ...
as she held you and kept you safe,
as she suckled you with the goodness of life,
as she wept for you, and kept smiling at you
to show you that love mattered above all else.

It was for your father to know ...
as he found new places to hide you,
as he made decisions on how danger could be avoided,
as he wondered if he'd failed to help you survive,
as he offered protection when he had little himself.

But now, in the fullness of your humanity, you know ...
you have heard of their pain and faced your own terror;
you have known of their uncertainty and experienced your own danger;
you have been cast down by their fear and lived with your own confusion;
you have wept in their lonely places and confronted your own death.

My human Christ,
be, now, a mother to me ...
Hold me and keep me safe.
Suckle me and feed me with life's goodness.
Weep if you must, but smile upon me too,
to show me that love matters above all else.

My human Christ,
be, now, a father to me ...
Hide me in your loving arms.
Shield me from present dangers.
Reach out from the fullness of your broken humanity
and offer me the protection of an Incarnate God.

My human Christ,
you are near me in my pain;
you comfort me in my times of terror;
you console me in my uncertainties;
you are beside me in my dangers;
you give me peace in my fearfulness;
you bless me with clarity in my confusions;
you are my companion in my loneliness;
you fill me with hope in the face of my mortality.

My human Christ,
I need your humanity
to help me make sense of mine.

Why should we be so kind?

(A hymn inspired by Ruth 2:10)

> *This hymn was written in response to the refugee and migrant crisis in
> Europe. A refugee, Ruth found understanding, welcome and compassion
> from Boaz, a rich and influential landowner. She is scraping grains of corn
> from a field as she follows the harvesters, and Boaz offers her 'more than
> she expects'. She responds, 'Why should you be so concerned about me?
> Why should you be so kind to a foreigner?' (Ruth 2:10, Today's English
> Version).*

Tune: 'This joyful Eastertide' (CH4 415)

Why should we be so kind
to those who're running scared from fear and danger?
Are we to love inclined
when others would reject the frightened stranger?
To love is God's command;
to love, our way of living,
this truth to understand –
it's God's own love we're giving, we're giving,
we're giving, we're giving.

Why should we be so kind
to those with ways as foreign as their language,
with faces deeply lined
with pain and sorrow, brokenness and anguish?
It's Christ who bids us go,
some fuller lives to fashion,
and in our welcome show
a glimpse of His compassion, compassion,
compassion, compassion.

Why should we be so kind
to those who bear the scars of accusation,
who're forced to leave behind
their homes, their peace, their families and their nation?
God's Spirit leads us on
as we, its light receiving,
will swell the Spirit's song –
'In Love's power we're believing, believing,
believing, believing.'

Why should we be so kind
to those whose eyes for mercy yet are pleading,
rejected and maligned,
whose hope in life and love is still receding?
For yet more love we pray,
to live, God's smile observing.
When kindness is our way,
God's purposes we're serving, we're serving,
we're serving, we're serving.

Freedom

Freedom from ...

persecution,
fear,
restriction,
discrimination,
war,
famine,
hopelessness ...

Freedom to ...
know peace,
raise a family,
find work,
find self-esteem,
worship as I choose,
speak out again,
be ...

Freedom with ...

acceptance,
hopefulness,
purpose,
education,
people I love,
people who love me,
meaning ...

Freedom and ...

nurture,
belief,
faith,
security,
democracy,
love,
me.

Those who are now like me

I was discriminated against
because of my sexuality,
my religion,
my circumstances,
my postcode,
my status,
the colour of my skin.
So I turned in on myself,
and found hatred,
and bitterness,
and resentment,
and anger
deep within me.

But when I turned outwards again,
and saw others discriminated against
because of their sexuality,
their religion,
their circumstances,
their postcode,
the colour of their skin,
their stateless status,
I remembered what I had felt,
and knew they could feel hatred,
and bitterness,
and resentment,
and anger, even towards me.

So I determined to learn from my own past
and break the cycle of discrimination,
and accept those who are different,
and understand those who have varied religious practices,
and be sensitive to those whose troubled circumstances
have shaped their lives,
and be aware of postcode lotteries,
and see beyond skin colour,

and accept the refugee and stranger as if they were my own people – because I remember how it felt.

When hatred is challenged by grace,
when bitterness gives way to acceptance,
when resentment is overtaken by forgiveness,
when anger is calmed in the face of love,
I am the better for it,
and so are those who are now like me.

A lesson from a refugee: the story of Gerry Black

When I was a student in Edinburgh in the late 1960s and early 1970s, the issue of refugees didn't impinge much on my city or my life. I knew about refugees, of course. News reports in the press and on TV were informative and distressing. But the refugees were always in another place, a different country, a foreign land. I didn't have people from Afghanistan, Syria, Iraq – and all the other places in our present-day consciousness – on my own doorstep. Refugees were for other nations, other cultures, other governments to be concerned about.

What we did have, however – and what had a huge impact on an eighteen year old student from a relatively protected background – was a crisis of homelessness. There were 'no-go' areas of Edinburgh, peopled by 'dossers' and 'winos', tramps and rough-sleepers. And fifty years ago, they were victims of the same labelling, scapegoating, ignorance and prejudice experienced so often by our modern-day refugees.

So I share with you a story from my student days of a homegrown refugee.

Gerry Black had been a basket-maker. But that was in the days before chainstores, mass production, foreign imports and ubiquitous plastic. So making baskets was a thing of the past for Gerry, a thing of the long-distant, almost forgotten past. 'Gerald Black, Esquire, Bespoke Basket-maker' had been the sign over his well-stocked shop in Edinburgh's Stevenson Street, the outside festooned with quality wicker baskets of all shapes and sizes and for every purpose under the sun. But that was now a hazy memory, and the shop, like the street itself, had been long since demolished to make way for expanding university accommodation. For the truth of it was, Gerry Black had been down on his luck for many, many years.

It wasn't the reduction in the bespoke basket trade that had been Gerry's downfall, nor the demolition of his shop and all the others that had filled the streets and alleyways of his part of the city. That had been the start of it, right enough. But the drink, family break-up, time 'inside' and failing health had done the rest, and it had done plenty of damage to Gerry Black.

Homelessness for Gerry had become a way of life. Homeless men were figures of revulsion, labelled 'dossers' and 'winos', and to be avoided at all costs. Indeed, there were parts of the city which had been left to become the favoured haunts of the city's homeless, most of whom, unable to get a bed in a Salvation Army hostel or a Lodging House Mission, were reduced to sleeping rough – 'doing an outsider' – in the alleyways, shop doorways, stairs and backyards of the city's undesirable areas.

To be honest, I hated the dossers. 'It's their own fault,' I would intone. 'No need to be like that,' I would pronounce. Indeed, like most people, I would go out of my way to avoid them, and if, by chance, I came across one late at night when I was on my way home from the university library, I'd quickly cross the road for fear of contamination from one of the city's low-life. It was about the only thing that had disturbed me about the city which had become my student home. Everything else was great. But dossers and winos were a blight on a beautiful city and a horror in my own life.

That's why I find it hard to explain why I became friends with Gerry Black. It started when I was waiting for a bus and saw a bedraggled old figure emerge from an alleyway next to the bus shelter. I was about to dismiss the pathetic figure as 'another dosser' when I realised that the old man was carrying a bundle of canes under his arm. I watched with growing fascination as the old man divested himself of his mangy coat and laid it carefully on the pavement at the corner of the street. He sat down and, placing his bundle of canes by his side, deftly pulled out three strands and started to plait them together.

I couldn't quite make out what was going on, but I could see clearly enough that something was taking shape in a craftsman's hands. Whatever it was, before it was completed, it was laid carefully on the pavement while the old man rummaged in the pocket of his coat. Extricating something with obvious glee, he returned to his creation, somehow incorporating his new find into the object of his attention. Then, the work done, he snipped off the ends of the canes with a knife, also retrieved from his coat pocket, and held the finished object in front of his face to inspect it carefully. He shook it from side to side, and I realised that what the old man had made was nothing other than a wickerwork baby's rattle – the rattle made from his canes; the rattling noise coming from three beer bottle-tops.

That was the first of many rattles I watched Gerry Black make over the next three years. For I got to know Gerry very well indeed. Arthritis in his fingers meant that Gerry could only do one or two rattles a day, and, even then, they didn't bring in much money. But he was a proud man, and felt that begging was beneath him. Selling rattles was fine; begging and offering nothing in return was not. He would never take money from me, even though I pressed him often enough. And that's why I accumulated more wickerwork baby's rattles with bottle-tops in them than I'd care to admit.

Gerry Black had no place to lay his head. He was a refugee from all that I took for granted. I would often think of the old man 'doin' an outsider' while I was tucked up in my warm student flat. I would think of an old basket-maker in his 'glory days, when life wis braw', and think of him sitting on his coat at a street corner, reduced to making rattles for children. I would think of a society that had rejected Gerry Black – and many others like him – and wondered where things had gone wrong.

When I returned to the university for my final year Gerry Black was nowhere to be found. During the first few weeks of term I searched his usual haunts, but I never saw the old basket-maker again. No one I spoke to knew what had happened to Gerry Black.

I have a major regret about those days. I didn't keep any of Gerry Black's rattles. I wish I had, but they probably wouldn't pass the 'health and safety' test for my grandchildren anyway. But, when they're big enough, I'll tell my grandsons about Gerald Black, Bespoke Basket-maker, and make sure they know what a city can do for an old, master craftsman and all refugees.

I wrote a song about Gerald Black when I was a student. It's fifty years old now. I've added a few more verses in recent days. Who is the Gerald Black for us as we face the refugee issue today?

Discarded

A song for Gerry Black

Down through the West Port and into the Market,
see old Gerry come shuffling along,
old shoulders covered with faded grey overcoat,
wondering why the nights are always so long.

'Tell me, old man, have you eaten this morning?'
'Naw, son, ah huvnae eaten a bite,
fur ah huvnae nae money nor bed tae lie doon on.
Ye see, that's why ah did an ootsider last night.'

> *O God, keep you safe, my friend, old Gerry Black.*
> *No one makes rattles for children like you.*
> *Where, where will this great Festive City end up*
> *now old Gerry Black has gone too?*

Your fingers are bent; your canes are all broken;
you're only fit to make rattles now.
And the people walk by and pretend they don't see you;
they leave you there to get by on your own anyhow.

'There once wis a time ah made baskets fur gentry.
Aye, son, but things are no whit they were.
The canes that they gie me are just fit fur firewood –
ach, my son, d'ye really think that it's fair?'

> *O God, keep you safe, my friend, old Gerry Black.*
> *No one makes rattles for children like you.*
> *Where, where will this great Festive City end up*
> *now old Gerry Black has gone too?*

Down through the West Port and into the Market,
all through the Cowgate and up to the Tron,
no one comes shufflin' with faded grey overcoat,
no one makes rattles here now that old Gerry has gone.

And who will remember the worker who's worthless,
discarded by gentry, ignored by the crowd,
broken and twisted like canes that are useless?
'Just fit fur firewood' – for him, it's his only reward.

> *O God, keep you safe, my friend, old Gerry Black.*
> *No one makes rattles for children like you.*
> *Where, where will this great Festive City end up*
> *now old Gerry Black has gone too?*

And now as I sit at my chic pavement table,
amidst trendy wine bars, a city in song,
surrounded by people, all bent to their pleasure,
I still see an old basket-maker come striding along.

For now he walks tall, with the bearing of affluence,
a prosperous gentleman, so they all say.
It's Gerald Black, Esquire, Bespoke Basket-maker –
'Ach, son, sit doon, an' ah'll mak' ye a rattle the day.'

> *O God, keep you safe, my friend, old Gerry Black.*
> *No one makes rattles for children like you.*
> *Where, where will this great Festive City end up*
> *now old Gerry Black has gone too?* [2]

Some websites and resources

Focus on Refugees: https://ctbi.org.uk/new-website-focus-on-refugees/

Glasgow Refugee Asylum and Migration Network:
https://gramnet.wordpress.com/

https://www.refugeecouncil.org.uk/

The Red Cross: www.redcross.org.uk

UNHCR: http://www.unhcr.org/uk/

World Refugee Day: http://www.un.org/en/events/refugeeday/

Sources:

1. From UNHCR Mission Statement:
    http://unhcr.org.ua/en/contact-us/basic-facts/27-basicfact

2. Story and song adapted from 'The basket-maker', in *A Blessing to Follow: Contemporary Parables for Living,* by Tom Gordon, Wild Goose Publications, 2009

Living water

Some worship resources

Various contributors

Opening responses:

Creator Spirit, wellspring of our lives,
as the refreshing rain falls on the just and unjust alike
REFRESH US WITH YOUR MERCY,
WHO KNOW OUR OWN INJUSTICE.

As a stream flows steadily on,
defying all the odds of stone and water,
FLOW OVER EVERY BOUNDARY AND BORDER
THAT SEPARATES US FROM EACH OTHER.

As the waters of our baptism washed us and welcomed us,
RENEW US NOW IN NEWNESS OF LIFE AND UNITY OF LOVE.

As we were once held in the waters of our mother's womb,
HOLD US IN THE POWER AND PEACE OF YOUR ABIDING PRESENCE.[1]

Kathy Galloway

Prayer:

Lord, I am so comfortable;
the water is running out of our tap,
while so near us,
just a short bus journey away,
there are thousands of families
who don't even have a single drop.

When will the rains come?

Lord, try to open my eyes
to these basic needs of my brothers and sisters.
Keep me from being complacent:
let me not just turn on our tap
and forget their desperate need.

When will the rains come?

Lord, you do not see us as rich and poor,
but as one family,
involved with one another,
bearing each other's burdens,
going the extra mile, being concerned.

When will the rains come?

I don't know when they will come,
nor do the villagers,
but I do know that I could care more,
and maybe that by caring more,
my brothers and sisters will find new strength
even when the wells are dry.[2]

Peter and Dorothy Millar,
Iona Community members who lived for years in India

Some suggested Bible readings:

Genesis 21:14–19; Exodus 15:22–27, 17:1–6; 1 Kings 17:10; Psalm 107:4–9, 33, 35; Matthew 10:40–42; John 4:7–10

Water is life: A reflection from Uganda

Water, water everywhere! The opposite to my home country.

The pilgrimage leader asked me at Loch Stonaig on Iona if I would say something to the gathering about the water situation in the country which I came from and was returning to, Uganda.

As we stood on a small island near a clean-water loch which had supplied Iona for years with fresh water, I was pleased to share something of the contrasts between home and Iona.

Uganda is a landlocked country. Mains-piped water is only available in the major urban areas. 80% of the population of Uganda live in rural areas which lack adequate water supplies for domestic, animal and plant use.

People have to collect water from wells, springs, boreholes or rivers. Some of these sources have been used by both animals and humans, creating a hygiene problem. In the end, this causes waterborne diseases like diarrhoea, bilharzia, typhoid and cholera.

Long distances are often walked to access the water sources. Water collection is mainly done by small children and women using containers. A lot of time is spent at water points due to large numbers of people waiting their turn. There are no big water storage tanks in rural areas, hence water has to be used sparingly, which is a huge problem in the dry season.

Shortage of water has created the existence of a nomadic group of cattle-keepers commonly known as *balaalo*. The nomads move with large herds of cattle in search of water and pasture, disrupting the traffic on roads, destroying people's gardens. Land conflict between cattle-keepers and farmers has become rampant due to water shortage. Crops die or wither away during the dry season. We rarely have irrigation facilities. Crops can be grown during rainy season only. There is a big problem with global warming: the dry season has become longer, creating famine.

Water is life, no matter which angle one views it from, and the memories of that day at Loch Stonaig remain with me as I continue my life in Uganda, longing to return to Iona one day, if it is God's will.[3]

Patrick Obiga, in Masindi, Uganda
Patrick is a former volunteer with the Iona Community.

Water-cooler conversations: 'I'll drink to that!'

> *These three interwoven monologues can be acted out. This piece was written in response to extensive roadwork being done in our locality to replace water and sewage pipes; it can be adapted for your own locality.*
>
> *Voice A: commuter, smartly dressed, holding a china teacup*
>
> *Voice B: middle-aged woman, holding a large earthenware vessel*

Voice C: academic type, holding a plastic water bottle, speaking as though finding interesting bits in a book and reflecting on them for anyone who cares to listen

Bible reading: The woman at the well (John 4:5–14)

Voice A: They are digging up Main Street now – the traffic's terrible! It took me 20 minutes longer to get home today! …

Voice B: When I was little I used to love coming here with my grandma, the walk made shorter by her wonderful stories. There was always a crowd of kids to play with whilst the women drew the water and gossiped. Happy days, easier times …

Voice C: Some of the names of Britain's rivers are the oldest surviving names we have. The Celts would throw their finest metalwork helmets and swords into rivers they revered as sacred. I wonder if that's why people still toss coins into wells and pools for good luck? …

Voice A: Just today – it was so hot – and it's not like my car's got air-con! We were all sitting there, cooking in the traffic jam – so why does one idiot think he has the right to jump the queue? Shot off on the wrong side of the road. Nearly smashed into a motorbike coming the other way! You should have heard the language …

Voice B: When they started gossiping about me, I didn't want to come here any more. It was none of their business which men I was with; and I never took anyone else's husband. But that didn't stop them knocking over my water jars and shoving in front of me in the queue – and the things they said! It was easier to get my water when no one else was around, even if it was in the heat of the day …

Voice C: Purification rites are central in world religions: ritual making one clean, holy; giving protection from all that might endanger the soul. Water is used to bless, cleanse and purify. In some religions, waterways are believed to be the route to the afterworld. People still scatter ashes on the Ganges, don't they …

Voice A: You've got to admire United Utilities' P.R. team: I'd been stopped by one of their signs, the one with the picture of the fish: it got me thinking. I mean, we're lucky really, aren't we? Clean water on tap. We take it for granted …

Voice B: So you see, I didn't expect to meet anyone at the well, never mind a man on his own! At first I thought it was a set-up, another nasty trick, but it wasn't. He was different. He challenged me, but in a good way. He made me see myself differently. He got me thinking …

Voice C: Rivers and glaciers have shaped and formed our landscape. Our seas and lakes and rivers provide a rich source of inspiration for painters and poets alike. A fresh fall of snow, or a summer rainstorm, has children squealing with delight! The awesome power of Niagara Falls, or the gentle sounds of a garden water-feature, can inspire wonder and bring a moment of contemplation …

Voice A: I'd been grumbling about the traffic, and about the amount of rain we've been getting – but without sewers and a reliable water supply – well, just look at all those places where they still live like that – in 2017! That can't be right, can it? …

Voice B: And he *did* challenge me – to go back to all those women and tell them about him! But it was OK, it wasn't hard … well, a bit hard at first; but I didn't care that they laughed at me, I'm used to that. And they soon stopped laughing when they met him too …

Voice C: They are hunting for evidence of water on Mars and on some of the moons in our solar system. Water holds the key to life. Where there is no water, no living thing can survive. I wonder if there's life on Mars …

Voice A: Water: all of life depends on it. So when I got home, I googled Water Aid, and, well, I'll drink to that! *(raises cup, freezes in position).*

Voice B: 'Living water', he called himself; said all of life depends on him.

Well, I know mine does, and I'll drink to that! *(raises vessel, freezes in position).*

Voice C: Mystical, spiritual, beautiful, precious water – I'll drink to that! *(raises water bottle; then all three women move away).*

Elaine Gisbourne

Affirmation:

God who created heaven and earth,
AND FOUNDED THE LAND ON DEEP WATERS.
God who flooded the earth
AND GAVE US A PROMISE.
God who divided the water
AND SET THE PEOPLE FREE.
God who leads us beside still waters
and gives us new strength:
WE AFFIRM OUR FAITH IN YOU.

Jesus who walked on water
AND CALMED THE RAGING SEA.
Jesus who turned water into wine
AND BAPTISES US WITH WATER, SPIRIT, LOVE.
Jesus who washed his disciples' feet
and washes our souls clean:
WE AFFIRM OUR FAITH IN YOU.

Holy Spirit who is poured out
AND COMES TO US AS WATER AND FIRE.
Holy Spirit who is strength and power
AND FILLS US WITH YOUR LIVING WATER.
Holy Spirit who is gentleness and love
and is God's gift to each of us:
WE AFFIRM OUR FAITH IN YOU.[4]

Author unknown

Closing responses:

A blessing on you who are poor
YOURS IS THE KINGDOM OF GOD.

A blessing on you who mourn
YOU SHALL BE COMFORTED.

A blessing on you who thirst for justice
YOU SHALL BE SATISFIED.

A blessing on you who make peace
YOU SHALL BE CALLED THE CHILDREN OF GOD.[5]

Blessing:

May clean, clear water bless us,
wellspring or waterfall,
life in abundance
flowing, cleansing, refreshing.

May we use wisely God's gift of water
and cherish each drop;
bring life to earth's deserts.

Jesus, pour your water,
greening and satisfying,
on the dry dustiness of the deserts within us.

Holy Spirit, flow through us;
revive our faithfulness,
cleanse our sinfulness,
fill us with prayerfulness.[6]

Chris Polhill

Suggestions for action:

www.wateraid.org/uk/
www.christianaid.org.uk
www.wellsforindia.org

Sources:

1. From *The Pattern of Our Days: Liturgies and resources for worship from the Iona Community*, Kathy Galloway, Wild Goose Publications, 1998

2. © Peter Millar. Used by permission of Peter Millar

3. From *Around a Thin Place: An Iona pilgrimage guide*, by Jane Bentley and Neil Paynter, Wild Goose Publications, 2011

4. From *Holy Ground: Liturgies and worship resources for an engaged spirituality*, by Helen Boothroyd and Neil Paynter, Wild Goose Publications, 2005

5. From *Iona Abbey Worship Book*, Wild Goose Publications, 2001

6. From *Eggs & Ashes: Practical and liturgical resources for Lent and Holy Week*, by Ruth Burgess and Chris Polhill, Wild Goose Publications

About the authors

Tim Aldred is an associate member of the Iona Community. He has worked for international development charities for most of his career, and is currently Head of Policy and Research at the Fairtrade Foundation. He lives in Bromley with Sally and their two daughters.

Dave Broom is a teacher and a former member of the Iona Community's Resident Group on Iona, where he worked as Sacristan in 2012.

Ruth Burgess is the author of many books and resources, including *A Book of Blessings*, *Eggs and Ashes*, *Hear My Cry*, *Fire and Bread* and *Winter* (Wild Goose).

Ian M Fraser has been a pastor-labourer in heavy industry, a parish minister, Warden of Scottish Churches House, an Executive Secretary of the World Council of Churches, and Dean and Head of the Department of Mission at Selly Oak Colleges, Birmingham. He is the author of numerous books, including *Strange Fire*, *The Way Ahead*, *A Storehouse of Kingdom Things* and *Reinventing Theology* (Wild Goose). Ian is one of the original members of the Iona Community who helped George MacLeod to rebuild 'the common life' and the Abbey buildings on the isle of Iona. Throughout his life Ian has travelled the world, alone and with his wife, Margaret, visiting basic Christian communities. He has walked alongside slum dwellers in India and Haiti; Nicaraguan and Cuban revolutionaries; priests, nuns and catechists facing arrest and/or death in Central and South America; and small farming and fishing communities in the Philippines.

Kathy Galloway is a member of the Iona Community.

Elaine Gisbourne is a member of the Iona Community living in Lancaster. She is a physiotherapist, working in a local hospice, as well as a Spiritual Director, Street Pastor and campaigner for world development issues.

Tom Gordon is a former hospice chaplain, storyteller and member of the Iona Community. He is the author of several books, including *Look Well to This Day: A year of daily reflections*, *A Blessing to Follow: Contemporary parables for living*, *Welcoming Each Wonder: More contemporary stories for reflection*, and *With An Open Eye: Parables with meaning for today*. Two of his books are based specifically on his experience as a hospice chaplain: *A Need for Living: Signposts on the journey of life and beyond* and *New Journeys Now Begin: Learning on the path of grief and loss*.

John Harvey was a member, with his wife, Molly, of the Gorbals Group Ministry in the 1960s, and a parish minister in Gorbals, Govan, and Raploch in Stirling. He was Warden of Iona Abbey for five years in the 1970s, and Leader of the Iona Community from 1988 to 1995. He has been a member of the Iona Community since 1964.

Ruth Harvey is the Director of Place for Hope (www.placeforhope.org.uk), a Scottish-based mediation agency working with faith communities and churches. Place for Hope offers training, coaching and conflict accompaniment to groups, individuals and networks. Their support helps churches and faith communities to embrace conflict, navigate difficult conversations well, reach solutions, and work through transitions. Ruth is a member of the Iona Community, a Church of Scotland minister and a Quaker.

Janet Lees is a URC minister and a speech therapist, and has been Chaplain at Silcoates School in Wakefield since 2010. Her two books, *Word of Mouth: Using the Remembered Bible for Building Community* and *Tell Me the Stories of Jesus: A Companion to the Remembered Bible*, as well as several shorter digital downloads, are published by Wild Goose.

Glendon Macaulay was a Church of Scotland minister in Falkirk where he took particular interest in working (often ecumenically) with congregations to encourage and develop innovative and creative worship styles. He is the author of *Dirt, Mess and Danger* (Wild Goose Publications).

Joy Mead is a member of the Iona Community and the author of *The One Loaf, A Telling Place, Making Peace in Practice and Poetry, Where Are the Altars?, A Way of Knowing, Words and Wonderings, Glimpsed in Passing* and *Walking Our Story*. She leads creative writing groups, and has been involved in development education and justice and peace work.

Elisabeth Christa Miescher is a member of the Iona Community living in Switzerland.

Peter Millar is a former warden of Iona Abbey, who has worked in India, Glasgow, Africa and Australia. He is the author of several books, including *An Iona Prayer Book* (Canterbury Press), *Finding Hope Again* (Canterbury Press), *A Time to Mend* (Wild Goose Publications) and *Our Hearts Still Sing* (Wild Goose Publications).

Patrick Obiga lives in Uganda and is a former volunteer with the Iona Community.

Chris Polhill is a member of the Iona Community and one of the first women priests in the Church of England. She has contributed to a number of Wild Goose books and is the author of *Eggs and Ashes* (with Ruth Burgess), *A Pilgrim's Guide to Iona*

Abbey, A Heart for Creation and *In the Mists on the Shoreline*. She and her husband, John, run the Reflection Gardens, which highlights the Christian spiritual journey and environmental issues.

Rosemary Power is a member of the Iona Community who has been in pastoral, sector and congregational ministries; and is the Iona Prayer Circle Coordinator. She writes and speaks on the history of Iona, spirituality and issues of social justice.

David Rhodes worked as a national newspaper journalist, before his ordination as an Anglican priest. In the 1990s he joined the ecumenical project Faith in Leeds and began running his innovative 'retreats on the streets' to help Christians make the vital connection between their faith and social justice issues. He is the author of *Faith in Dark Places, Finding Mr Goldman: a Parable, Sparrow Story* and *The Advent Adventure* (SPCK). He is an associate of the Iona Community.

Thom M Shuman is the author of *The Jesse Tree: Daily Readings for Advent, Gobsmacked: Daily Devotions for Advent* and *The Soft Petals of Grace: Communion Liturgies and Other Resources,* and is a contributor to many Wild Goose anthologies and downloads. He lives in Columbus, Ohio and is an associate member of the Iona Community.

Jan Sutch Pickard is a poet, preacher and storyteller living on Mull. She is former Warden of Iona Abbey, Vice President of the Methodist Conference, and Ecumenical Accompanier. Her books and many resources include *Out of Iona: Words from a Crossroads of the World* and *Between High and Low Water: Sojourner Songs*, and *A Pocket Full of Crumbs* (Wild Goose).

Kathryn Turner has worked in prayer and spirituality for over 25 years and is particularly interested in getting resources into people's hands that are accessible and help them to deepen their relationship with God. She is a member of the worship group Wellspring, and is a contributor to many Wild Goose anthologies.

Wild Goose Publications is part of the Iona Community

- An ecumenical movement of men and women from different walks of life and different traditions in the Christian church
- Committed to the gospel of Jesus Christ, and to following where that leads, even into the unknown
- Engaged together, and with people of goodwill across the world, in acting, reflecting and praying for justice, peace and the integrity of creation
- Convinced that the inclusive community we seek must be embodied in the community we practise

Together with our staff, we are responsible for:

- Our islands residential centres of Iona Abbey, the MacLeod Centre on Iona, and Camas Adventure Centre on the Ross of Mull

and in Glasgow:

- The administration of the Community
- Our work with young people
- Our publishing house, Wild Goose Publications
- Our association in the revitalising of worship with the Wild Goose Resource Group

The Iona Community was founded in Glasgow in 1938 by George MacLeod, minister, visionary and prophetic witness for peace, in the context of the poverty and despair of the Depression. Its original task of rebuilding the monastic ruins of Iona Abbey became a sign of hopeful rebuilding of community in Scotland and beyond. Today, we are about 250 Members, mostly in Britain, and 1500 Associate Members, with 1400 Friends worldwide. Together and apart, 'we follow the light we have, and pray for more light'.

For information on the Iona Community contact:
The Iona Community, 21 Carlton Court,
Glasgow G5 9JP, UK. Phone: 0141 429 7281
e-mail: admin@iona.org.uk; web: www.iona.org.uk

For enquiries about visiting Iona, please contact:
Iona Abbey, Isle of Iona, Argyll PA76 6SN, UK. Phone: 01681 700404
e-mail: ionacomm@iona.org.uk